Letters to a New Teacher

LETTERS TO A NEW TEACHER

*A MONTH-BY-MONTH GUIDE
TO THE
YEAR AHEAD*

JIM BURKE
WITH
JOY KRAJICEK

HEINEMANN
PORTSMOUTH, NH

Heinemann
361 Hanover Street
Portsmouth, NH 03801–3912
www.heinemann.com

Offices and agents throughout the world

The authors and publisher wish to thank those who have generously given permission to reprint borrowed material:

Excerpts from *The Cure at Troy: A Version of Sophocles' Philoctetes* by Seamus Heaney. Copyright © 1990 by Seamus Heaney. Reprinted by permission of Farrar, Straus and Giroux, LLC.

"The Seven of Pentacles" from *Circles on the Water* by Marge Piercy. Copyright © 1982 by Marge Piercy. Used by permission of Alfred A. Knopf, a division of Random House, Inc.

"Ask Me" and "The Way It Is" from *The Way It Is: New & Selected Poems* by William Stafford. Copyright 1977, 1998 by the Estate of William Stafford. Reprinted with the permission of Graywolf Press, Saint Paul, Minnesota.

"The Abnormal is Not Courage" from *Monolithos* by Jack Gilbert. Copyright © 1982 by Jack Gilbert. Used by permission of Alfred A. Knopf, a division of Random House, Inc.

Ethos Diagram from *Public Speaking* by Michael Osborn and Suzanne Osborn. Copyright © 1988 by Houghton Mifflin Company. Used with permission.

(Acknowledgments for borrowed material continue on p. xx.)

Library of Congress Cataloging-in-Publication Data
Burke, Jim.
　　Letters to a new teacher : a month-by-month guide to the year ahead / Jim Burke with Joy Krajicek.
　　　　p.　cm.
　　Includes bibliographical references.
　　ISBN 0-325-00923-6 (alk. paper)
　　　1. First year teachers.　I. Krajicek, Joy.　II. Title.
　LB2844.1.N4B87 2006
　371.1—dc22　　　　　　　　　　　　　　　　　　　　　　　　2005027449

Editor: Lois Bridges
Production: Abigail M. Heim
Typesetter: Kim Arney Mulcahy
Cover design: Judy Arisman, Arisman Design Studio
Cover photography: Steve Bernier
Manufacturing: Steve Bernier

Printed in the United States of America on acid-free paper

10　09　08　　　　　VP　　　　　3　4　5

To three essential colleagues,
mentors, and friends:

Sandy Briggs,
Elaine Caret,
and Diane McClain

The Inheritance

—baloian

You become the student
the open book on a desk
a constellation
passing from one room to another
through a tempest of memory and years
a legacy you hold in your hand
like a star

A shepherd
you gather
in the lost ones
mend broken wings
and shipwrecked hearts
Finally the pages
of the book
begin to blanket
the landscape
and among the words
green spears
of wildflowers
begin to populate
your life

Note: baloian is a poet who also teaches English at Burlingame High School. He wrote this poem on the occasion of our colleague Marilyn Nelson's retirement.

Contents

⌒

- Writing as a craft
- Advice from the masters
- Advice from the students
- The importance of writing about meaningful topics
- The apprenticeship model
- Students as authors
- Revising ourselves

- Teaching is good but *hard* work
- Improvement through revision
- What master teachers do
- Becoming a resilient teacher
- The courage to teach
- Doing what makes a difference

NOVEMBER

- The importance of personal reading during the year
- Be an interesting person and an example to your students
- Making time to read
- Benefits of poetry
- Teach different types of texts
- Seek opportunities for personal and professional renewal
- Orientation • disorientation • new orientation
- Reflect on work and life
- A letter to the young teacher I was

SPRING SEMESTER

Foreword

⌐⌐

Over the past few years, we have been involved in creating spaces where teachers can reflect on their relationship to the vocation of teaching. The stories we have been privileged to hear are about men and women struggling to make sense of the good and bad days of classroom life. They yearn to be teachers who bring light and life to their students and they often suffer from working in schools where the resources and support are nowhere near commensurate with the challenges. We have been especially honored to spend time listening to novice teachers describe the crazy quilt of experiences and emotions that characterize their first years in practice.

To sit with young teachers as they speak of their struggles, triumphs, and questions is to be reminded that teaching is no mere technical endeavor, but an expression of one's heart, one's fiercest passions, and one's humanity. The noted jazz critic Joseph Feather once said that listening to Billie Holiday was like listening to the "voice of living intensity of soul." To hear beginning teachers describe their work, their lives, their aspirations, their fears is to listen to that same voice.

Despite the raw, haunting quality of this voice, we wonder whether it is being heard. We know that teachers enter this profession for reasons of the heart. They come with an ethic to serve the young and with a desire to make a difference in the world. They show up ready to contribute, but too often find themselves isolated in their classrooms and working within institutions lacking in collegiality, professionalism, and administrative support.[1] The upshot of these conditions is a staggering attrition rate where almost 40 percent of new teachers leave the profession in the first three years of teaching; by the fifth year almost half are gone.[2] When teachers leave the profession,

---

1. R. M. Ingersoll, *Who Controls Teachers' Work?: Power and Accountability in America's Schools*. Cambridge, Mass.: Harvard University Press, 2003.

2. National Commission of Teaching and America's Future, *No Dream Denied: A Pledge to America's Children*. Washington DC: National Commission on Teaching & America's Future, 2003.

they do so wounded by the conditions that left them unable to realize their initial aspirations. When there is a revolving door of new and inexperienced teachers in a school it becomes nearly impossible to develop the professional habits found in cohesive learning communities. In the end, children suffer because their teachers do not stick around long enough to develop and hone the skills, knowledge, and understandings that good teaching requires.

These problems pose fundamental challenges to our society and demand multidimensional policy interventions. But teachers on the ground working day after day in our nation's classrooms can't wait for grand policies to make sense. They must find ways to survive and thrive in the here and now. New teachers are particularly vulnerable to being overwhelmed by the sheer intensity of the emotional and intellectual labor, and they are in urgent need of support and sustenance that understands the poignant mix of issues facing neophytes in their work.

Such support and sustenance is the great gift offered by this exchange of letters between first-year teacher Joy Krajicek and master teacher Jim Burke. Joy's courage in opening her heart and sharing her questions, her predicaments, her fears and vulnerabilities allows us to begin to understand the "intensity of soul" that is teaching. Her verve and desire to serve her students and honor her profession embody what we believe are the values that new teachers bring to the work. As she tells Jim, "I have the passion to be a great teacher and feel so wanting of the tools."

We can almost taste her desire to learn to do the work of teaching well. She hungers to know what Jim teaches, how Jim teaches, for what purposes he teaches—and how, amidst all the demands and pressures, he maintains his passion for the work. One cannot read her questions and responses without appreciating her desperation to learn enough to survive, to thrive, to do right by her kids.

In the face of Joy's great need, Jim offers us a vision and model of what it means to be a mentor to a new teacher. Joy yearns for the tools, the techniques, and the right methods with which to bring order and routine to the first year of teaching. Jim understands this and provides ample suggestions for how to organize your room to deal with talkative students or how to structure a lesson on the essay. His ability to provide clear, cogent advice on what to teach and how to teach is a great asset for Joy and for the readers of this book—but that is not what makes this collection of letters remarkable. What Jim ultimately offers Joy and every reader is a vision of what the teaching profession can and should become.

Jim offers Joy a vision of teaching grounded in skillful means, collaboration, continuous learning, *and* an abiding sense that good teaching cannot be reduced to technique but comes from the identity and integrity of the teacher. Jim offers Joy a way of becoming a teacher that includes an ongoing love affair with English and writing: a model learner who seeks out colleagues who can make him better; a student of his own teaching who can simultaneously lament his failures and learn from them; and, lastly, a man who appreciates that he is at his best as a teacher when he can call upon the intellectual, emotional, and spiritual resources that emerge from who he is.

Joy's questions and Jim's responses evoke in us an appreciation for what it means to do the work called teaching with the "living intensity of soul." May such soulful teaching flourish among us: here is a book that can help it be so.

Sam M. Intrator and Parker J. Palmer

Acknowledgments

Once it became apparent that these letters spoke to a larger audience I began showing them around, testing them out on trusted colleagues and those readers of my other books who would write for advice. This helped me to gain better focus in the letters as I wrote and thought about how people would read and use them.

Along the way certain people offered important confirmation as to the value of the letters and made suggestions for how I might improve them. Penny Kittle, Sam Intrator, and Amy Wevodau provided instrumental guidance; I am most grateful for their insight and friendship. Kate Montgomery, a fellow ex-Peace Corps volunteer who wrote a book of letters (with Hilary Liftin) about that experience (*Dear Exile: The True Story of Two Friends Separated (for a Year) by an Ocean*), became a regular reader of the "Joy letters" after her initial comments offered essential help in understanding how such letters should be organized. Many thanks for her enthusiasm and comments. I also appreciate the many new teachers with whom I began to share the letters, often in response to some pressing question not unlike those Joy asked. They made helpful suggestions and affirmed the value of the letters.

My deepest gratitude is reserved for Lois Bridges, my editor at Heinemann. It was through a book of letters that I once wrote to a student and her mother that Lois and I came to know each other. That book was called *Fellow Travelers* and was, I now realize, not a book that deserved to be published. But it led to our relationship, to her invitation to write about my experience in the classroom. She has been my fellow traveler ever since, giving me the opportunity to become the writer I always dreamt of being. As I began to show Lois these letters she responded with genuine enthusiasm and appreciation for what the letters accomplished. In this way, the letters here, though written to Joy, marked for me something of a return to a form (the letter) through which I had developed my craft as a writer. For it was through letters, while living in Tunisia in the early 1980s, that I learned to describe the world to a woman who would eventually become my wife. Thus I end, as always, by thanking my wife, Susan, for without her I would never have become a writer.

(Continued from p. iv.)

Introduction:
Living the Questions

You are so young, so much before all beginning, and I would like to beg you, dear Sir, as well as I can, to have patience with everything unresolved in your heart and to try to love the questions themselves as if they were locked rooms or books written in a very foreign language. Don't search for the answers, which could not be given to you now, because you would not be able to live them. And the point is, to live everything. Live the questions now. Perhaps then, someday far in the future, you will gradually, without even noticing it, live your way into the answer.
—Rainer Maria Rilke, from *Letters to a Young Poet*

On the first day of school a young woman walked into my classroom as my third period was ending and introduced herself, telling me her name was Joy. She was, she said, a brand-new teacher and would be teaching sophomore English at our school. Thinking about the troublesome statistics about new teachers who leave the profession early, often because they do not feel supported, I told Joy that if she had questions about *anything* related to teaching and working at Burlingame High School, she should jot them down on an index card and give it to me before I left that day. My motives were simple and small: to help a new teacher by jotting a quick note on the back of an index card, rather like a postcard. However, Joy asked questions that from the beginning challenged me to think about what it means to be a teacher, questions that resisted a three-by-five-inch answer.

My first letter was ten typed pages long.

Each letter I wrote seemed like it would be the last. After all, I was busy teaching my own classes and tending to the needs of my own family at home. Then another question would come and inspire new insights and the desire to reflect on teaching in a more personal way than my other books have allowed. Finally, something of a rhythm established itself: every few weeks, Joy would give me a card. And a few times she sent me an email when a question was more urgent or needed more space than an index card would permit. The questions evolved into a list of essential questions any new teacher would ask, posed in the order in which they naturally occurred to Joy over the course of the year.

She would usually hand me a card as I stuffed papers into my briefcase, punctuating the gesture with a grin and a comment such as "If you get a chance . . . I had a question for you." I usually read her latest question before I began my drive home; thus my mind could begin working on her new question right away. Driving along, I jotted ideas down on the pad in my car. By the time I got home thirty minutes later, I was often ready to write.

The letters here appear in the order in which I wrote them. Most were written in a sitting and usually delivered to Joy within a day or three of receiving her question. Instead of putting the letters in her hand or sending them through email, I made a point of putting the letters in her box in the main office. We rarely talked about them and certainly never considered that we were writing a book.

This last point is important: While these letters speak to any teacher, they were written to Joy as private letters, as a form of personal professional development, as part of an ongoing conversation between us that became, through these letters, a very rich personal meditation on our work as teachers. We had one mostly unspoken rule that was important: Joy did not have to respond. New teachers face a swarm of demands already; feeling compelled to respond to such long letters would have made the correspondence a burden, not a blessing. Too often efforts to help new teachers translate into additional obligations that burn them out instead building them up. I mention this to explain the absence of letters from Joy throughout the book. It also makes her few letters that much more welcome: you hear her voice emerging as the year unfolds.

I began to realize these letters would appeal to a larger audience when I read excerpts from a few of them at a convention where I was speaking about what it means to be an English teacher in the twenty-first century. When I finished speaking, new teachers came up to say how much they appreciated hearing the letters. They all said the same thing: "I thought I was the only one who felt that way." Indeed, they might have written what Joy wrote after I offered to stay late and observe her class on certain days:

> I realize that I should ask you to come visit my fourth period. However, I am filled with fear about having you come in. Fear of what you might find and fear that I am some horrible teacher that has no idea about what I

am doing. I think I have some guilt complex because I tend to think the worst if someone has something to say to me—that I've done something wrong or offended them. This transfers to observations of my teaching and so on. Ahhh! So, I am not quite ready to have you come in. Nonetheless I am going to try and work up to it.

I admit I grew to love getting Joy's questions. They became assignments to go off into the hills and think about the work I love so much. Over time, there was, for me, a feeling that various conditions had conspired to make this correspondence and our relationship the perfect opportunity for such an exchange. Moreover, many people might feel awkward or intimidated if someone wrote ten pages for every one question they posed, but Joy seemed to understand that I benefited from the letters, too, and that her questions were not a burden. She just gave herself permission to ask and listen and reflect.

When I wrote my last letter to her at the year's end, a great sigh went through me. I had long dreamt of writing a book of letters, one similar to Rilke's *Letters to a Young Poet*. In that book, Rilke writes to the young poet seeking guidance: "There is only one thing you should do. Go into yourself. Find out the reason that commands you to write; see whether it has spread its roots into the very depths of your heart; confess to yourself whether you would have to die if you were forbidden to write. This most of all: ask yourself in the most silent hour of your night: must I write?" Joy asked us both a question we spent the year trying to answer: Why do we teach? And from that came other questions: What does it mean to be a teacher now? What kind of teacher am I? And, to borrow from Rilke: Must I teach?

We spent the year wrestling with these questions, "living the questions," as Rilke writes elsewhere. I was never Joy's teacher but always her colleague. And so we offer these letters, these questions and responses, to you to help you meet the challenges you face in your own classroom or school, but also to help you better understand why you teach and what kind of teacher you are or are striving to be. As you begin to find the answers to these questions, remember to turn around and offer a hand to those coming up behind you: they need your wisdom as much as you need their wonder at the complexity, importance, and beauty of our work.

Jim Burke

Question 1

How do you manage a group of thirty-five sophomores who won't stop talking and pay attention?

∽

Dear Joy:

Of course nothing frustrates us more than when the students don't sit there like angels and take in every word we say or engage in every activity with the eager love of learning we imagined when we created that lesson the night before. And talking seems especially upsetting to us at times because our teaching is inevitably an expression of ourselves, our values, our commitment to our work. So we often experience their talk as a rejection of *us*, and that never feels good.

Stephen Covey, author of *The Seven Habits of Highly Effective People*,[1] says we must seek first to understand and *then* to be understood. This principle helps me often as a teacher since I am not fourteen, nor a student who is required to attend school, nor a student who finds himself asked to do what he feels he cannot. Thus when an intrusive behavior interferes in my classroom, I must ask myself why. Sometimes the answer helps; other times it hurts because I realize I have to accept that I am part of the problem. I find myself often returning to a list of essential human needs I picked up along the way from Frank Firpo, a legendary master teacher from our school; these needs, which help me reflect on my own teaching and the extent to which I am meeting the kids' needs, include

comfort

safety

control

tradition

friendship

nurturance

recognition

success

independence

variety

curiosity

enjoyment

Often I find that the cause of trouble is that I am not—perhaps because I don't know how—meeting some crucial need that the disruptive student has. Of course when you have thirty-five students in one class, there are a lot of needs; how can you possibly know—or *meet*—them all? As the poet William Carlos Williams wrote, "The virtue is in the effort." So I try, and I let the kids know I am trying to understand them, and when in doubt, I *ask* them what they need; by doing this I meet one need we all have, which is to be listened to.

I had a girl last year who was having all sorts of trouble in class, which I eventually found out stemmed from the fact that she wasn't eating. I had another kid who seemed unable to stop talking, but a lot of his talking came from a daily routine of hustling the class till he had "borrowed" enough money to get something to eat and thus satisfy his physical need for food. As it happened, he was also adopted and thus seemed to feel a serious need to belong and to feel accepted by his peers. This turned out to be true for a number of kids in my class who talked constantly: one boy, I later found out, had been in forty-two foster homes by the time he'd entered my ninth-grade class; one girl moved between parents and relatives, never feeling accepted anywhere but at school, and so passionate was her need for friends and social acceptance that she could not easily find the strength to then care about school except when her grades got so low that it threatened her friendships (i.e., if she failed, she would be moved to the alternative school and thus lose her friends). There are, in these exciting days of education, other explanations for the pathology of talking; for example, attention is in short supply among many kids these days, and I don't just mean those with ADD or ADHD.

I guess my point here is that kids talk and act out for different reasons. My guess is that you were a pretty good student, one who behaved the way you wish all your students would. There is an old saying among Christians: Hate the sin but not the sinner. Well, talking isn't a sin, but it's a pain; nonetheless, as you work on solving the problem, try to keep your heart open to the kid as a person even as you work to change them as a student.

Still, you want some nuts and bolts ideas to try, something to *do* that might help. Here are a few things I and others have tried over the years. You can choose the ones that make the most sense in light of your kids, your classes, and their needs:

- *Establish clear rules from the beginning and enforce them consistently.* Kids need boundaries. One of the hardest things for many teachers, especially new ones, is to be tough. We like kids and don't want to be the bad guy. We want them to like us but also respect us. We want to be one of those teachers they tell stories about years from now because in some way we changed them, helped them improve.

- *Reward appropriate behavior and punish inappropriate behavior.* This suggestion is filled with loaded words, of course. *Punish*? This can mean something as simple as letting those who finish their work have time at the end of the period to get started on their homework or read for pleasure, a positive consequence that punishes those who haven't finished (because they were talking).

- *Have a chat.* I routinely take kids aside for quick chats to find out what is going on and to help them understand the effect their behavior is having on the class. This provides the attention they often seek and gives me some insight into their individual needs.

- *Reevaluate your assignment* in light of the Four Cs of Academic Success. The Four Cs—commitment, content, competencies, and capacity—allow us to quickly assess students' readiness to complete the assigned task. Joey or Amanda might be talking because they simply do not have the content knowledge or skills needed to do the assignment; in that case, I realize I need to do some teaching—perhaps for a few students or the whole class—so they can do what I thought they were ready to do. Or, they may not know what a successful performance looks like on this assignment; then I need to provide a model from a past student or create one myself, showing them how I would do it. (For more on the Four Cs, see Appendix C.)

- *Tell them where to sit.* This might mean changing their seat. It might mean telling them which group they can and cannot work with. It might mean arranging the class in alphabetical order on the first day so that you are not doing anything personal to them—Hey, your last name is Kinavey; that's just where you happen to sit. It's nothing personal, Mr. Kinavey.

- *Make an agreement.* This might mean telling them that if they work well in this group or on this assignment today, you will let them work with a group of their own choosing next time; it might also mean telling them that you have the referral slip written out and this is their warning (before the bell has even rung), and at the first instance of disruptive talking, you will have to ask them to leave. "It won't be personal, Miss Jones; it's just that we have a lot of important work to do today and there's no time for interruptions." Or, if you need to pull out the big guns, fire one across their bow and say, but not in an angry or threatening way, "Mr. Ames, give me your best today. I know you have a lot to offer and that talking is sometimes getting in the way of your success. I might have to give your parents a call if you keep it up."

- *Exit cards.* This technique gives the kids a chance to write anonymously to you about how things are going and ways they could be improved. Just pass out index cards near the end of the period and ask them to identify ways the class could be improved and how you might go about implementing those changes. If kids see that you actually listen to them and try to act on some of their suggestions, they will work better and have more respect for you.

Whatever you do, try always to treat the students with respect. Don't let them bring you down to their level. It can be too easy to blame all our bad days on that one kid or group of kids and not look honestly at ourselves, our lessons, or our techniques. Learning is, after all, inherently social, so try to create structured, productive contexts for students to do work that requires them to talk. This is rather like the ancient martial art of aikido, which, as I understand it, suggests using your opponent's moves and momentum to defeat them; if you have kids who are very social, give them cause to be social but at the service of their learning. Yesterday, for example, I had kids get into groups to have a discussion about and create the rules for tragedy. This led to a lively but productive discussion about whether their friend in middle school who killed himself was a tragic figure and whether the divorces that a number of their parents had gone through were, in fact, tragedies. This then prepared them for further rich (and academic!) discussion in the second half of the period, during which they applied their criteria for tragedy to Hamlet to explain why he was or was not a tragic figure.

When I watch the way you greet your kids as they come in and the way you talk to them, I can't help but think how lucky they are to have you,

Joy. You are obviously committed to their success. These qualities are not incompatible with being strong and demanding also; watch Diane McClain across the hall sometime and you will see a master whose love for her kids is as deep as it is demanding. She says all the time that the "kids are the enemy," but when you watch her, you see that she abides by the ideal that we should love our enemy. She is the teacher we all strive to be: tough, funny, memorable, nurturing, and intelligent—all at the same time. There's so much to juggle if we are to be the teacher we see in our imagination.

Your colleague,

Jim Burke

P.S.: I have attached something I call the Action Planner. I use it to help me analyze and solve problems. I thought you might find it useful. (See Appendix B.)

Question 2

Do you have any creative ideas for teaching a unit on
House on Mango Street?

Dear Joy:

I like the fact that you build your question around the word *creative*, because that is what I love most about teaching: it is creative. Artists begin with a blank canvas, musicians start with blank tape, writers sit before the blank page (or screen!) and dream up the people, places, and plots they will create through words. And we teachers create, but with what? And what, exactly, do we create? Nancie Atwell, one of the profession's genuine masters, writes:

> I confess. I started out as a creationist. The first days of every school year I created, and for the next thirty-six weeks I maintained the creation: my curriculum. From behind my big desk I set it in motion; then I managed and maintained it until June. I wanted to be a great teacher—systematic, purposeful, in control. I wanted great results from my great practices. . . . I didn't learn in my classroom. I tended my creation. Today I learn in my classroom. What happens there has changed, and it continues to change. I've become an evolutionist. The curriculum unfolds as my kids and I learn together and as I teach them what I see they need to learn next.[1]

How does this relate to your question? In a few ways. First, I don't tend to think in terms of teaching a unit, so much as in terms of creating conversations inspired by the books we read or the subjects we study. It's an important difference to me, because in this climate of standards-based instruction (most of which I support, within reason), we are always in danger of losing sight of why we want kids to read, write, or talk about anything other than some identifiable standard. So what is it we create in our classes? Conversations. Opportunities. Encounters. Experiences. Knowledge. And what are these made from? Ideas, words, texts, images. And what are these "units" made of? Vocabulary? Story structure? Tests and quizzes about literary terms and plot details? Books we bring into our classrooms are made of stories, images, and voices that we must help students learn to hear and to enter into conversation with so that they may come to better understand not only the books and the characters but the world within and around the students.[2]

It so happens that *Mango Street* is a rich collection of voices and stories that everyone in your class can relate to, have fun with, and learn from. First, it's about neighborhoods. Everyone has lived in at least one, and every neighborhood is nothing but an anthology of stories that reside in houses, trees, backyards, and secret places. Have kids generate a list of people, places, events, and memories and give them room to tell those stories and to hear others' tales the way people have always sat around and told stories: in circles. When I did this with *Mango Street*, someone would mention some story about a crazy neighbor or the time the bank robbers came on their street, and then certain common memories would emerge: "Ohmygod, remember when the clouds of butterflies came out of the sky in fifth grade?" The kids can draw to prepare to discuss, and discuss to prepare to write, and write to prepare their own stories to be read aloud. Memories are also made up of people, and the stories that go along with those people. I try to share something of myself with the kids on such occasions, partly to model for them; so I will make a list of a bunch of names they don't know and then circle, say, Terri Freitas, who was my baby-sitter when we lived on Thirty-sixth Avenue, and tell them about how she was my first love (even though I was eight) and nothing has ever been as sublime as sitting in a circle on her front lawn on a summer evening, looking on in wonder as other bigger kids sat telling stories while they passed around a box of Milk-Bone dog treats and crunched them up. Kids might say, "But what about me? I live in an apartment building," or "We moved a lot." What's an apartment building but a vertical neighborhood? And what are a bunch of different neighborhoods but a collection of stories that can all be blended into one long neighborhood that spans the world they have traveled?

Then when the kids are getting into their voices, using *Mango Street* as a model, you can drift into the whole spoken aspect of the text. It begs to be read aloud, something you need to learn to do as an English teacher, for it not only helps kids understand better but builds a community within the classroom as it takes them back to that ancestral place where we long to gather around the fire to tell the stories of who we are or long to be, where we've been or hope to go. The acting group Word for Word adapted *Mango Street* into a series of brilliant dramatic vignettes and performs them word for word as they were written. Making room for the kids to perform certain portions of the text builds community and gets them reading and talking about the story.

What, then, have I said in response to your question? I've said that you need to give kids a range of ways to work with and appreciate a text like *Mango Street*—reading, writing, talking, and representing to different audiences for various purposes—and much of it should be social and thus more engaging. Doing this makes it much easier to build bridges between a text about a thirteen-year-old Latina in Chicago and everyone in your suburban classroom in California who might be, on the surface, different from Esperanza. The activities I just outlined would allow me (as a suburban white guy) to write a *Mango*-like story about Ken, the vet who spent all day in his yard working on cars and building a kayak after returning from the war when I was a kid, or Carmen, the woman who took in everyone's laundry on our street, or Tom Dundis, the terror of my neighborhood, whose mother seemed always to be sitting in the front room quietly talking to nuns and priests while her son was abusing all the kids on the block in various sadistic ways.

Is this pedagogically sound? Sure. Here are Judith Langer's six features of effective literacy instruction, which are based on years of research:

- *Feature One*: Students learn skills and knowledge in multiple lesson types.
- *Feature Two*: Teachers integrate test preparations into instruction.
- *Feature Three*: Teachers make connections across instruction, curriculum, grades, and life.
- *Feature Four*: Students learn strategies for doing the work.
- *Feature Five*: Students are expected to be generative thinkers.
- *Feature Six*: Classrooms foster cognitive collaboration.[3]

I know what you are thinking: That's a lot to do! Of course this is what makes our work so fascinating and complex: the simultaneity of it all. That is why you need to give yourself permission to try to do a few things well and add new elements to your routine as you are able. Think about those jugglers at the fair: they don't get it all going at once. Rather, they get two, then three, then four things going; and when they are ready, they tell the kid in the audience to toss them the apple, the saw, or the monkey to add to their juggling routine. Am I saying don't do vocabulary or grammar? Of course not. I'm just saying to pick the few things that will help you and your kids feel most successful ASAP so you can keep alive the good feeling of community you have grown this first week in your class. Worry about the sustained silent reading (SSR) next month or the month after that, when you have your rhythm going strong and steady and are ready to add something new and different; after all, variation is one of those essential needs I told you about in that last letter.

This brings me to my last point for tonight's letter. Now is not the time to go into depth about this, but this morning when I asked you how your weekend was, you joked that you "have no time for weekends!" At the risk of overusing the juggling metaphor, let me return to it briefly. This work of ours will never get simple and never, as Nancie Atwell said earlier, get under control. We work in the midst of barely controlled chaos. You must set aside time for yourself on the weekends and each day during the week (even if it's only fifteen minutes!) to tend to your own needs. This is how I began reading poetry again. It's why I listen to books on tape. Because our work is never done, we can always be working. And then it consumes you and the next thing you know you lose your joy of teaching, and you join the ranks of the 60 percent who leave the profession within their first five years. You must teach yourself the habits that will allow you to sustain not only your love of teaching but your love of life.[4] You are only what . . . twenty-five? You must, as hard as it can be, give yourself permission to get up from your desk and go into the garden, out to the beach, over to a friend's, or out to dinner for conversation about things other than teaching and school. This is essential to your personal and professional health. When you look at Diane McClain, you see a woman who has taught for thirty years, has raised kids on her own as a single parent, has made time to become a great golfer, still reads, goes to plays—and still is a great teacher. To be an interesting teacher you must get out and live life and bring that example and those stories into your classroom. Otherwise, you will end up like Esperanza in *Mango Street*, sitting in the window, thinking that life is elsewhere.

I have gone on longer than I expected, but your questions get me thinking. One last thing, and not a small one: I love the way you begin class every day by telling the kids it's important to settle down and get ready to work because they have "many important things to learn and do today." It's a great way to begin and sets the right tone. It also reminds you of what I have tried to say here in too many words: this is important work, and your commitment to doing that work well comes through. I'm sure the kids appreciate it.

Your colleague,

Jim

Question 3

Am I the only one who is weighed down by the pressures I alone set for myself?

⌒

Dear Joy:

Your recent letter raises several important and fascinating questions about the relationship between teachers and students, and the nature of our work in general. I would like to say that all teachers share the sense of vocation, the passion for the work that we both clearly feel; it is not true, however, which is why it is so important to seek out and participate in the kind of conversation we have begun. It is essential that we find experienced guides not only to help us find and keep to the path we have chosen but to show us that it is possible to love this work for as long as we choose to do it. Writing of happiness, but also about much more, the philosopher Seneca wrote:

> First, therefore, we must seek what it is that we are aiming at; then we must look about for the road by which we can reach it most quickly, and on the journey itself, if only we are on the right path, we shall discover how much of the distance we overcome each day, and how much nearer we are to the goal toward which we are urged by a natural desire. But so long as we wander aimlessly, having no guide, and following only the noise and discordant cries of those who call us in different directions, life will be consumed in making mistakes—life that is brief even if we should strive day and night for sound wisdom. Let us, therefore, decide both upon the goal and upon the way, and not fail to find some experienced guide who has explored the region towards which we are advancing; for the conditions of this journey are different from those of most travel. On most journeys some well-recognized road and inquiries

made of the inhabitants of the region prevent you from going astray; but on this one all the best beaten and the most frequented paths are the most deceptive. Nothing, therefore, needs to be more emphasized than the warning that we should not be like sheep, follow the lead of the throng in front of us, traveling, thus, the way that all go and not the way that we ought to go.[1]

I learned early on the value of finding such guides and turning to them, as you have done to me and, in the past, to others such as your mentor teacher, to ask them questions. Nothing made a bigger difference. It was through such conversations with Steve Poling, a colleague at my first school, that I learned how to think about stories and how to teach them. And it was through Pat Hanlon, my master teacher during my student teaching program, that I learned how to teach, how to think about what I taught, and how to love my work by making it my own. I began teaching when I was roughly the same age you are, though in a very different environment than the one we teach in now. As a senior in college I took an internship at a private school for kids with severe developmental disabilities and psychological disorders. By giving myself permission to submit to master teachers like Lois Yaroshefsky, Gary White, and people whose names now fade with time's passing, I learned about not only teaching but kids, for the first thing my colleagues all taught me was to love the kids, even when they were difficult.

Some of my mentors, like Carol Jago, taught me early on that if I was to be the teacher I wanted to be, I needed to read, to find models in men and women whom I could study and thereby, through their ideas and their examples, become a master teacher like Carol was (and still is).

Your gifts for the work—both with the subject and with your students—are evident to me from the moment you walk in the classroom every day. Your concern about your age, your lack of experience, how you measure up to people like your master teacher and others—these concerns are misplaced and ignore your gifts. Keep these "doubts of inadequacy," as you call them and these nagging fears that you will not be perfect, but keep them only to the extent that they help to push you harder to be better. I have learned to trust my feelings of anxiety, my fears that I will fail, for I have come to realize that it is that commitment to my craft, that conscience about the quality of my work, that keeps me working at the lesson longer to make it better. You ask if others are "weighed down by the pressures" of the work, and the quick answer is, of course, yes. But a more complex answer might be no or sometimes. Those blessed by the curse of conscience about their work, who strive to be craftsmen, artists, masters, find within the work that burdens many a feeling of blessing, a well of energy, what Don Graves calls "the energy to teach."[2] When he was writing his book about this subject, Don asked me to study myself for a week, to investigate my energy: what sustained it and what drained it, and why. It was a revelation to me.

I suspect Don would find this energy in people in any profession who feel called to do the work that fills their days. This is the nature of work as *vocation*. Not only does such work seem to give voice—for that is the root of the word *vocation*—to our true self, but through our work, we often seem able to help others find their own voice, to discover who they are, their gifts, and how they can contribute. The poet William Stafford writes, in a poem called "Vocation," that our job is "to help the world find what it is trying to be."[3] An experience I had the other night captures what I mean by all this. Colleen McNally, who was a freshman in the first class I ever taught, emailed to say she was going to be in town and asked if she might come visit. It had been fifteen years, but we had kept in touch after I moved to another school and she entered college and eventually graduated with her doctorate in psychology. Her visit was wonderful, but what stood out was her comment about the role I had played in her life, the influence I had exerted simply through my commitment to her success as a person and a student. If we are lucky, and effective, if we take the best part of our work seriously, we become what I have apparently been for Colleen: one of the voices in each student's head that speaks to them, reminds them who they are, what they can accomplish. I should emphasize the words *one of the voices*, for as Diane McClain says so often, "we are all just one piece of the puzzle."

I prefer to think of us not as pieces of the puzzle, but rather as characters in the stories our students will tell about their lives. We can be major characters or minor ones, heroic characters or villains. In this way, I find I must always regard what I do *now* through the window of a future that is far away. I must wonder, of all that I am teaching, of all that we are doing, all that they are studying, what will remain, what will find a place in the story of their life, especially that story they will tell about who they are and how they discovered and shaped that identity.

I don't think we can—or should—set out to become such a character in students' lives. Instead, I think we must know our own gifts and make use of them in the most authentic, powerful ways we can. What I do may not work for you, but here are a few tactics I use to get to know and try to reach the kids I teach:

- *Say hi whenever I see them in class and around school.* I must confess, it would never occur to me to not say hi, but after a girl mentioned it in her graduation speech, I realized how ignored kids often feel around school. I talked to a student one time last year who said that after nearly a semester, one of her teachers still did not even know her name.

- *Talk to kids about their interests.* I hate heavy metal music, but I love talking to Tyler Gamlen about his band Reflections of Ruin and their CD cover in all its horrid, gruesome details because it's who Tyler is, what he wants to be; if I can't meet him where he is, he won't follow me where I want him to go (as a student). If Miguel is into skateboarding, I'm going to ask him about what tricks he's working on or how he got that scar. Through such conversations, we recognize their gifts and honor them by taking them seriously.

- *Touch kids.* This is obviously a dangerous thing to say in this day and age, but still I stand by it, with reservations. First, by touch, I mean giving high fives, handshakes, pats on the shoulder—whatever is appropriate and effective. And if I *ever* have doubts, I don't do it—for the kid's sake, and mine.

- *Write them notes.* This is my favorite thing to do. I keep a stack of index cards handy at all times (for various purposes). If a kid does something rare, makes a big difference in our class that day, or seems down, I will try to find time to scratch out a few sentences of praise, encouragement, or gratitude. A handwritten note is a written voice they can keep with them and reread long after your class is over. I have done this from the beginning without thinking about it, but after hearing from parents and kids about the difference such notes make, I became more intentional about it. When a boy's mother told me once that her son had one of my notes stuck over his desk at home as a reminder that he could succeed, I realized those quick notes were accomplishing a lot more than I expected or even intended. And when Colleen McNally mentioned at dinner the other night that I had written her a letter that she had kept these many years, I was amazed to hear her talk about it and the effect it had on her. She told me that in one of her graduate courses they had to bring in artifacts that represented different influences; when she read my letter to the class, she said everyone commented that they had never received such encouragement from a teacher.

- *Share.* If I am reading an article in the *Wall Street Journal* that I think Eric Showen will like, I bring it to school for him when I am done. When I finished reading the *New Yorker*, I give it, with the recommended article(s) circled, to the appropriate student, usually Rick Wiepking or Jessica Hwang this year, saying, "There was a great article in here I thought you might like since I know you are interested in . . ." If I read a poem I know a kid will like, I copy it and pass it along. Such specific sharing says that I know who they are, that I think about them, and that I'm interested in much more than their grade in the class. Sometimes sharing takes different forms: a band I think they might like, an art exhibit I saw, a movie I am sure they will appreciate, and so on.

Does this work for everyone? Do I do these things for all students at all times? Of course not. To borrow your own words from your last letter (which I thoroughly enjoyed), "I take a deep breath, try to calm myself, pray, and affirm my hopes of becoming the best educator possible as I continue to work hard and not lose sight of my purpose."

What you are doing will teach you to become the educator you wish to be. The Latin word *educare* means to draw out, which is what you continually do to yourself when posing questions to me and, through your letters, to yourself. It is this willingness to enter into the conversation about yourself and your work that distinguishes you—that, and the fact that you have the courage to do so *honestly*. It is that kind of commitment that will make you the kind of teacher John Steinbeck wrote about when recalling one of his teachers:

> In her classroom our speculations ranged the world. She breathed curiosity into us, so that each morning we came to her carrying new truths, new facts, new ideas, cupped and shielded in our hands like captured fireflies. When she went away, a sadness came over us. But the light did not go out. She had written her signature upon us: the literature of the teacher who writes on children's minds. Many teachers have taught me soon forgotten things but only a few like her created in me a new direction, a new hunger, a new attitude. I suppose to a large extent I am the unsigned manuscript of that teacher. What deathless power lies in the hands of such a person.[4]

Enjoy the week ahead. Back to School Night is this week. Let me know if you have any questions about that. And if you are here and want to join me and a few other wonderful teachers for dinner, we'd love to have you.

Your colleague,

Jim

P.S.: You should think ahead to the following year and realize that there will be at least one retirement and thus a full-time position open within the department. So throughout the year, even if by email, keep in touch with Diane and Marilyn (the department chairs) so they know you and what you have to offer when they choose a new hire next year.

Interlude 1
A LETTER FROM JOY ABOUT A DIFFICULT STUDENT

Dear Jim:

Thank you for your last letter. The comments and advice you gave were so pertinent to my "state of teaching" and they resonated deep down to my soul. It is easier to think about some of the things you said rather than do them; however, I will make an effort to practice what you recommended (especially since they truly fit, I believe, with my personality and style of teaching).

I have a question for you about a student I have at Mills High School. But first the setting: My fifth-period class is probably my most difficult or the one I feel the least confident in my teaching skills after spending time with them (luckily sixth period is the polar opposite, so I do not leave each day in shambles). This class has a wide variety of ability levels, reaching from the very talented, "should be in honors" kids all the way down to the attitude-problem, "I hate reading and English sucks" kids. A good percentage of my students are low performing and have difficulty with the play we are reading. I am using different methods to scaffold the unit and assist even basic comprehension of the play. Unfortunately the translation of Cyrano I used at Santa Cruz High School was much easier to read than the one Mills High School has. Add to this difficult class students who like to goof off and seem to have too many friends in class (turn my back from them and I am dead!).

Now, there is a girl, and I hate to admit this, but I sometimes wish she wasn't in my class. She challenges my confidence. Everything I am trying to do for her seems to numb her to any enjoyment of this class. She hates the play we are reading, won't read, disrupts class—well, she is constantly off task, doesn't pay attention (I have to really watch her so that I am constantly challenging her lack of attention with my helpful check-ins and simple presence close to her desk). I have pulled her aside, talked with her, expressed my thoughts nicely, complimented her, asked about how she is doing each and every day, and have planned activities hoping that she would be slightly more interested than she is any other day. So far she sometimes has a little better attitude, but otherwise enters the classroom hard and mean and leaves just the same. I don't know what to do!

I was talking to a student in my sixth-period class about how he likes the book and what he would like to do to make it more interesting for the class, etc. . . . . He then mentioned . . . this student I have in fifth period, the problem one. He said he had meant to warn me about her, that last year she was very difficult to handle for their English teacher. She didn't show up much (which is at least an improvement from last year), complained, gave attitude, and the like. The teacher was working so hard to improve the course for her, but to no avail. From what he knew, as he was a friend to her last year, she did not pass the course. Sadly he mentioned that I should not try too long to please her or ignite her curiosity. It would be no use.

All my strategies of trying to get to know her and discover the home life she has and how she is doing, what she likes, etc. have not worked. She responds OK to my attention in class and I am working so hard to pique her interest any way I can. Yet, she stated that once she hates a book she won't participate or enjoy anything we do. This is all killing me and she is often in my prayers and I am hoping to unlock her heart/mind so that I can truly understand what is going on.

Any advice? The class itself is already a challenging one and this girl is a thorn in my flesh. I hate to think of her that way, but she is troublesome for me. Help!

Thanks,

Joy

Question 4

I hate to admit this, but I have a girl I sometimes wish wasn't in my class. She challenges my confidence. WHAT SHOULD I DO?

Dear Joy:

I'm glad to see you trying things that will engage the kids but help them learn at the same time. The best evidence of your success in the class was the group of kids who stayed after class the other day to talk to you about their vignettes and just to be with you. When kids stay after the bell has rung, it speaks volumes. It reminds me of when I visited Mrs. Baldwin, my fifth-grade teacher, about ten years ago. I was driving by my old elementary school and realized it was just after school on a Friday. I loved Mrs. Baldwin, though I gave her no end of grief and was always being told, "If you do that one more time, Jimmy Burke, you'll be sent to the principal's office!" So I walked into Mrs. Baldwin's classroom, after what . . . twenty-five years? And the first thing I noticed was all the kids still hanging out in her room, all of them working away despite the fact that school had been out for nearly half an hour and it was a Friday. Then—I swear this is true—she turned and saw me standing in the doorway of the same room where I had been a student, and without batting an eye, she said, "Well, Jimmy Burke, what a pleasant surprise. Come on in." I had run into someone that day who had said she worked for my old school district, and when I asked if she knew Mrs. Baldwin, she immediately exclaimed, "Elaine Baldwin is a legend!" And when I saw the kids there after school, and saw myself returning twenty-five years later, I could only appreciate the truth of those words.

You wonder perhaps why I digress with such a story, but my point is that it is these experiences you want to create (students performing their vignettes in the park), these relationships you want to establish to ensure you will make the kind of difference for your kids that Mrs. Baldwin made for me. Years ago, when I first became a teacher, I wrote her to tell her I had become a teacher, though I assumed she had long forgotten me. She wrote back immediately to say that she had not forgotten me nor any of our class—because we were her first class! I could not imagine that she had been a new teacher, a novice, and yet she had made this lasting, enduring mark on my life that stays with me even today.

Sometimes, of course, things get in the way and prevent us from having such an impact on kids—or so we think. In your latest letter you brought up a few questions about frustrations and obstacles. Teaching is full of them. My first thought about your fifth-period class is that fifth period is often a . . . special class: right after lunch, early afternoon, some already thinking about what they get to (or have to) do after school, all of which is happening as the food (especially the sugar) from lunch catches up with them. The funny thing is that by year's end, it is precisely classes like these that we come to love because of all that we have been through together. They know they can be exasperating, and they love and respect you all the more for hanging in there with them, for not giving up on them, and for coming back day after day to try once again to start the fire in their minds. The best example I can give of what I mean and you are experiencing is from Carol Jago's book *Beyond Standards: Excellence in the High School English Classroom*. Here is Carol's opening page, in which she describes her fifth period. Remember, Carol Jago is one of the profession's true masters:

> My period five students enter the classroom with their mouths still full from lunch. Oscar arrives with a pizza box that attracts Jessica from the other side of the room. Cristina comes in laden with three bouquets of flowers and six helium birthday balloons. Matt and Ryan are roughhousing near the computers, but before I can tell them to watch out for the monitors, the bell rings. Not one of the thirty-six students in attendance pays a bit of mind. In case you were wondering, this isn't a third-grade classroom but twelfth-grade English, and my plan for the day is the study of Quincy Troupe's poetry. Employing every classroom management skill I know (and a few invented over lunch), I bring these pulsing teenagers to relative order.
>
> My students don't mean to make teaching difficult. They simply have 1,001 more important things on their minds than the lesson at hand. Or so they believe. My challenge is to create a bridge between a few of those 1,001 things and their class work. I use the word *work* here intentionally. Teachers err when we tell students that "learning is fun," though not because it can't be. The mistake is in placing learning in competition with pizza, flowers, and balloons. Lunch beats senior English every time. I know these students are capable of excellence, but it takes more than cheerleading on my part to help them achieve. It takes work.[1]

Carol has kids of all levels in this class, just as you do. She has kids that "hate reading and think English sucks," as you say of your kids. And certainly after some thirty years, she has a bigger bag of tricks than either you or I have. She has something you should have but sound like you worry you will lose: confidence. Some of this confidence stems from the inevitable blessings of experience: Carol overcame difficulties only to realize that she was successful after all. Some of this confidence, however, comes from knowing what she can get away with. For instance, if a teacher like Carol was strapped with the terrible translation of *Cyrano* that you have, she might do whatever she could to get a hold of that better translation you mentioned, even if it meant borrowing copies from another school in the district that had it. She would also realize, as I need to often remind myself, that the school year has its seasons, and some kids go fallow during certain of them. But all the while, the experienced teacher soldiers on, doing what you yourself say in your own letter: "using different methods to scaffold the unit and assist even basic comprehension of the text." They also look for ways to build a bridge (without dumbing things down) between the book and the kids' own experiences. For the record, this use of what they know about to help them connect with and understand what they don't is one of the three "key findings" of an important book titled *How People Learn*. The three findings are:

1. Students come to the classroom with preconceptions about how the world works. If their initial understanding is not engaged, they may fail to grasp the new concepts and information that are taught, or they may learn them for purposes of a test but revert to their preconceptions outside the classroom.

2. To develop competence in an area of inquiry, students must: (a) have a deep foundation of factual knowledge, (b) understand facts and ideas in the context of a conceptual framework, and (c) organize knowledge in ways that facilitate retrieval and application.

3. A "metacognitive" approach to instruction can help students learn to take control of their own learning by defining learning goals and monitoring their progress in achieving them.

The authors go on to identify three "implications for teaching," which are worth adding:

1. Teachers must draw out and work with the preexisting understandings that their students bring with them.

2. Teachers must teach some subject matter in depth, providing many examples in which the same concept is at work and providing a firm foundation of factual knowledge.

3. The teaching of metacognitive skills should be integrated into the curriculum in a variety of subject areas.[2]

No doubt you are thinking, "Yes, well, that's good stuff to know, *but what about this girl who hates my class?*" First, I won't pretend to have an answer that doesn't exist. All I can do is tell you what I have experienced and learned and let you draw from that what will help you with this girl and students like her. I always try to remind myself that there are so many possible reasons for kids to act like this girl, only a few of which I can even try to control. One year, for example, I had a boy named Mike who was a good kid made of hard materials: his was a face of stone and every assignment I gave, every comment I made seemed lost in the air, as if I had never spoken. Like the rain, I slowly wore him down—as you are doing with this girl—by never excluding him, never putting him down, always greeting him, every time approaching him as if *this* time he would do the work. At the end of the year, while pretending to take the final exam for a class he could not pass if God himself were to take the exam for him, Mike wrote me a moving letter that detailed the misery of his life at home, where his mother had married a man who caused him no end of grief. His letter went on to say that he had thought by failing all his classes he would "show her" but only now (that he had achieved his goal and was looking at a summer filled will summer school *and* a jerk of a stepfather *still* living with them) realized that he had made a terrible mistake. He went on to apologize for not doing the work and to thank me for never giving up on him and always making him feel welcome.

Another kid, a girl, wrote at the end of her year with me (during which she did little work and failed most classes):

I just want to wake up one day all grown up or at least 18 and not have to go to some boring school with people I barely know. As I think about my life, I realize how many people I don't know, how many people I didn't give that one chance you need to become someone's friend, how many people I judged before getting to know them. I don't care if some people don't like me, I don't care if people don't like the clothes I wear. I know some people are not going to like me no matter what I do or what I wear to make them like me, no matter how hard I try to be friends with them I won't make a difference or change their mind. I don't want to be friends with someone who doesn't like me. I am in the ninth grade now and it's time I change my ways. This is my freshman year. I don't judge people I don't know any more. I did myself a favor by changing my mind about the way I think about people. I do not judge by skin color or by the clothes they wear. I just judge by their attitude! This is the lesson I learned this year, my freshman year!

What *are* we to do with these hard kids? The poet Seamus Heaney writes in *The Cure at Troy*:

> Human beings suffer,
> They torture one another,
> They get hurt and get hard.
> No poem or play or song
> Can fully right a wrong
> Inflicted and endured.[3]

We have these kids who come into our classes, all of them different, some of them broken in more ways than others, each of them struggling—if not with reading or writing, then with loving or living. We learn these things as English teachers because our subject deals with the stories of who we are and wish we were; in our classes the text of the stories we study weaves with the text of the lives the kids live, and it is our job to somehow manage the complexity of these stories in ways that develop not only their literacy but their lives as well. And what do we have to work with? Stories and words mostly. Heaney says somewhere that "no poem ever stopped a tank," and he says in the previous excerpt, "no poem or play or song can fully right a wrong." But through that study of literature, the study of lives and language, understanding can sprout, insight into themselves and those who made them "hard" can be revealed—a *voice* can emerge. You are, after all, working with kids who are in the middle of some of the most confusing, tormented years their lives will ever know. They live in the eye of a tornado of confusion they help to create and use to sustain themselves. They fear standing out and looking stupid as much as they dread being a nothing and unknown, a nobody. Adrienne, a student I had last year, wrote the following in June while the class scattered across the baseball field to reflect on the year:

I have changed so much this year! I am a lot more outgoing. I remember one of my first English classes this year. We were asked one simple question about how you would improve a car. When Mr. Burke called on me, I became very shy and said someone already said my answer. This was not true. I just did not want to sound stupid. And now at the end of the year,

I have said some of the weirdest, stupidest things ever. I've grown from mistakes I made. I have made so many new friends. I think the biggest person who influenced me is Zak. Zak and I did not really get along in the beginning of the school year, or the middle—ha ha. But these last two months I have gotten to know him really well. He is so independent and he always says what is on his mind. I hung out with him for like an hour one Sunday and it felt like all day. He has so much to say that I have to just shut up. And, for me, that is so hard.

Now this is a nice, friendly girl, of course. Adrienne outshines the sun and was a joy to have in class. But what you notice in common with the other letter is the role of relationships. Adrienne had them; the other girl did not. Let me take you a bit further into the mind of a sophomore girl like the one you describe, a girl who was very stern, very hard, but whom I came to appreciate as the year went on—and oh, what a year. Her name was Katie, and reflecting back on the sophomore year in my class, she wrote:

This has been a hard year but it's finally over. As usual I told myself at the beginning of the year that I would do good in school. Now it is the end of the year and I am failing all my classes. I don't know if it is lack of motivation or just plain laziness, but whatever it is, it's keeping me from achieving my goals. I'm not even sure what my goals are anymore. English has always been my favorite subject. I never seem to agree with English teachers' curriculum, and maybe that's why I don't do work. I am very stubborn and I don't like to do anything I don't like or agree with, probably the reason for my bad grades. I liked English this year. It was my favorite class.

The beginning of the year sucked. Every year so far at this school was extremely disappointing. My English class last year was so pointless, I hated it, but I did my work anyways. I was looking forward to this class because Mr. Burke was going to teach it. Then I found out we were having a student teacher, and my chances of having a great teacher were shot. Though I felt bad for poor Miss Shrader, I didn't want her as my teacher. I think the whole class felt that way too. We wanted a real teacher. So we tortured poor Miss Shrader in order to get one.

When you walked into the class after she left everyone expected to get yelled at. Suddenly a class that couldn't pay attention if their life depended on it was totally silent, all eyes on the teacher. You didn't yell at us. From that time on, I totally respected you as a teacher and a person.

We finally became a class. A few people in our class acted like they came straight from pre-school. Our class underwent many changes, people left, people came, but our class was always a family. We were free to discuss whatever we wanted. We had intellectual debates, and our minds were finally stimulated.

Although I love English, I still didn't do all my work. I found out that I have trouble accepting help. My mom, my teachers, my counselors were always trying to help me, but I didn't accept any of it. I think I find it easier to wallow in self-pity and not try to change myself and slowly deteriorate.

This has been my best class ever. Unfortunately this year came to a sad end with the death [by suicide] of one of our family members in the last two weeks of school. Mikey brought so much to this class, but he left it all with us. Even though I hate this school, I loved this class. Thank you for never giving up on us.

I don't include this letter for its praise of my work but as a glimpse into the mind of the girl you mention and to show how kids' thoughts and feelings—about themselves, those around them, and the world in general—change like the weather over the course of the year. I feel as though I ramble and roam in this letter, but I'm trying to capture one of the essential complexities of our work, which I sometimes find best represented by one of the sayings from the *Tao Te Ching*: Do your work and step back.[4] In other words, you should come in every day prepared to be the best teacher you can be, and committed to that girl's success, and you should never stop caring about her, but you should not let her determine your success, nor should you teach to her needs at the expense of others. True, the Bible says it is best to take care of the sheep that strays from the path, even at the expense of the rest of the flock, but this is different: those other kids rely on you to be *their* teacher. They are ready, and as someone once said, when the student is ready, the teacher will appear.

Later on in the same poem I quoted earlier, Seamus Heaney writes:

> So hope for a great sea-change
> On the far side of revenge.
> Believe that further shore
> Is reachable from here.
> Believe in miracle
> And cures and healing wells.

I find this part of the poem important, for with kids like the one you mention, I need to persevere in my hope that they will change, if not with me, if not this year, then eventually, when they are ready; then I think about what I would want them to say when they think back to my class. I want them to say something like what Katie says above, I suppose.

When I reread your letter, all I hear is the evidence of change, of progress, such as when you write: "So far she sometimes has a little better attitude" and that she comes to class (compared with last year, when she cut all the time), "which is at least an improvement," and "she responds OK to my attention in class." Let me remind you of what you might have forgotten: this is the *fourth* week of the year, and already you see differences, improvements.

Sometimes teachers jokingly define a good student as one "who makes us feel like a good teacher." While I agree with that in an amused way, I see in you the courage needed to be this girl's teacher, of one who "believes that further shore is reachable from here." It is precisely this difficult aspect of our work that makes it so important, and such private, unobserved struggles that make it difficult for the public to appreciate the complexity of our work. One last story with a nice ending to help you see the long road we must all walk on our way to who we will become:

> Of all the things she told me, there was only one I remember, and that was that you are not expected to succeed. This was said to me by my mother. She was talking to me about education. She had asked me what was going on with my grades. Then she went off about "how do you expect to get anywhere if you do not do your work." Then she told me that the Latin race are the lowest race to accomplish their education to go ahead and finish high school.

This sophomore girl—her name is Gigi—struggled in all the ways she describes in this note. And she graduated. And I see her once in a while, most recently just this last week while I was sitting in Starbucks grading papers. She's twenty-five now, and the mother of an adorable boy, and when she talks to me it is about the importance of education, of being a good mother, and then she picks up her latte at the bar and walks out to her job as manager of a major chain home furnishings store on Burlingame Avenue, where she is respected and proud of all that she overcame on her way to becoming the woman she is. This is the story you are a part of, the story of not just kids like Gigi but this community, this society.

Have faith: in yourself, this girl, and all your students. I know you seek perfection, but such a noble quest demands patience and practice en route to the revelation that such perfection is elusive and, ultimately, impossible.

Your colleague,

Jim

Dear Joy:

I'm so glad you are back and feeling better. No doubt you felt worse when you found out that no sub showed up for you than you did while home on the couch with your chicken soup. Surely you needed a day or two off; you have been working so hard, running back and forth between schools, teaching different books for the same courses on different campuses; you must have moments when you think to yourself, "Didn't I already say that?" or "Am I doing this at Burlingame or Mills?" I hope I didn't embarrass you too much today when I had the kids give you a round of applause for doing such a great job these first five weeks. Those kids are clearly behind you and this is no doubt a result of your investment in your relationship with them.

Which brings up your note about the difficult student we discussed in the last letter. I am sure the talk you had with her made a difference. Kids like that girl often have no adults who show an active and honest interest in them, so whatever she says or does, I would bet my life that in her heart and mind she keeps your name and counts it precious. And while I hope she will just move ahead like a happy camper and succeed, you should not be surprised if she slides into old ways (which are not so old) at times; this is natural, for she is, through your help, learning to live a new way. The poet Marge Piercy has this one poem called "Seven of Pentacles" that says, "Live as if you liked yourself and it may happen." This is a complex aspect of our work: the study and shaping of the self through the study of others' stories. Piercy captures the complexity and majesty of the work in that poem:

> Under a sky the color of pea soup
> she is looking at her work growing away there
> actively, thickly like grapevines or pole beans
> as things grow in the real world, slowly enough.
> If you tend them properly, if you mulch, if you water,
> if you provide birds that eat insects a home and winter food,
> if the sun shines and you pick off caterpillars,
> if the praying mantis comes and the ladybugs and the bees,

then the plants flourish, but at their own internal clock.
Connections are made slowly, sometimes they grow underground.
You cannot tell always by looking what is happening.
More than half the tree is spread out in the soil under your feet.
Penetrate quietly as the earthworm that blows no trumpet.
Fight persistently as the creeper that brings down the tree.
Spread like the squash plant that overruns the garden.
Gnaw in the dark and use the sun to make sugar.
Weave real connections, create real nodes, build real houses.
Live a life you can endure: Make love that is loving.
Keep tangling and interweaving and taking more in,
a thicket and bramble wilderness to the outside but to us
    interconnected with rabbit runs and burrows and lairs.
Live as if you liked yourself, and it may happen:
reach out, keep reaching out, keep bringing in.
This is how we are going to live for a long time: not always,
for every gardener knows that after the digging, after
the planting, after the long season of tending and growth, the harvest
    comes.[1]

Thus I tell you not to think that this troubled student won't cause for you again the grief she did before, but to realize that this process of change—which is at the heart of all education—takes time. It also takes the patient commitment that you show to your students, this one in particular, for so many kids lash out, push away those who care about them, but they do so as a test of whether that person (in this case, you) *really* cares. It's hard sometimes not to assume that they simply see themselves as unworthy of such faith, such attention, even such love; they seem not to love and accept themselves and so they wonder why anyone else would feel these things.

I've long believed that our job is to find those kinds of problems that fascinate us most and spend our life living in the midst of them, contributing our part toward the solution of those problems. The mathematician might spend years living within some particular concept he is trying to understand and apply in a useful way. My friend Jonathan has spent years moving around inside the microscopic world of cells in a passionate but patient effort to solve the problem of cancer. My wife also lives in the midst of three delightfully complex problems named Evan, Whitman, and Nora;

while I certainly play my part in raising them, it seems that Susan decided early on that she would commit herself to—because she was fascinated by—the challenge of raising good kids, which is to say kids who grow up to be moral, interesting, intelligent, healthy people. I say all this by way of remarking that kids like this girl at Mills perhaps reveal your apparent gifts and calling.

What is difficult about teaching, however, is that such work as you will do this year with this student and most others may well go unrewarded within the story of this year. Sometimes we do not understand the difference our actions do or will eventually make for some years. This is perhaps, at least in part, because kids themselves often do not realize the difference we are making at the time; only later, when things turn out well for them, do they realize that people helped them get there. I was thinking about this very issue this week because I received a letter from a former student who, when I had him as a freshman, drove me crazy for much of the year. I have foremost in my mind an image of him in the early weeks of the class standing at the window of my class, folding paper into planes and nonchalantly launching them out the window into the yard below, one after the other from a squadron he had carefully arranged on his desk. This was an advanced class and a small one; I was so dumbfounded, I could only ask him to please stop and get back to work. Things improved over time as I learned to appreciate Alden and understand his particular needs. Here is his letter, which came two years after he moved to North Carolina:

> It's been quite some time since I last said hello. My life has taken a few turns as of late, but most are for the better. I recently transferred out of my regular high school which offered few challenges and I frankly saw little point in even attending. I made great grades, but didn't have to lift much more than a finger to achieve them. I realized that while staying there I could succeed and likely have wonderful grades to show colleges, I would lack elementary skills I would need to do well at those colleges. There were a few options I had for alternate learning environments, none of which I was very interested in. That was until my mom found out about the Early College at Guilford. It's a school funded by the county that has partnered with a local private college to give high school students an opportunity to take classes at college. Ninth and tenth graders complete the first three years worth of high school requirements at an accelerated pace, and then get to take actual college classes with other

"traditional" college students in their junior and senior years. For me, this means dueling college and high school classes (since I missed accelerated 9th and 10th grades), but it's not a problem since they are all taught on the Guilford College campus.

The reason I was thinking of you was that my mom was nagging me to send thank you notes to people who had recommended me for Early College and helped me to get in. The application process included references, a plethora of questions, but most importantly, a three-page essay. I wanted to thank you for everything you taught me that allowed me to write this essay. I really didn't learn much in tenth grade, and wrote with the skills I learned in your class. Not only that, but you saw the potential I had in me and helped me to bring it out. I'd probably still be stuck at Western right now if it weren't for you. Thank you.

Alden Mueller

A letter like this would have seemed unimaginable to me when I had Alden. It's why I appreciate so much the time he took to write it; for this year I may have another Alden, and his letter reminds me that I am working inside the mess of an individual's evolution, that I must have faith not only in my methods but in myself and, most importantly, in that student. On the few occasions when I find myself in a casino (I never play because I *always* lose), I always imagine that those little old ladies working away at the slot machines, the women whose hands are black from the hours spent yanking that handle, are retired teachers who believe, who *know*, if they just hang in there long enough, their efforts will pay off. I can't resist sharing one other letter, one that above all others surprised me because you just don't expect kids you send to jail and get kicked out of school to thank you for it. I'll let the letter, which the student wrote at the end of his senior year, say it all:

Dear Mr. Burke,

Remember me? That's right, it's Jesse Arnold. Yeah, you remember, the kid that came into your freshman English class a couple of years ago after smoking a few blunts. OK, so maybe it was a very, extremely idiotic thing to do; but still this letter is supposed to be written to the person in my life that had the most impact on my educational experiences.

You, Mr. Burke, have definitely had more to do with my education than anyone. I remember it like it was yesterday. So me and my friend Joe decided to use the extremely genius idea of semi-cutting P.E. We would get dressed and then go to the wrong baseball field and smoke a little bit then go back, admitting that we went to the wrong baseball field, expecting a simple slap on the wrist. Instead, we ended up smoking weed for about forty-five minutes straight and when we got back to PE not only were we even more confused now that we smoked but to our dismay we were already fifteen minutes late to our next class.

That is where you come into the story, Mr. Burke. I come into your English class, which I was already struggling to pass, ten or fifteen minutes late. Before I say any more I just want to fully explain to you how obviously blunted I truly was; I barely knew where I was by the time I sat down, and by that time I already saw you writing a note which would soon be in the hands of Mr. Ryan, the assistant principal, in a matter of minutes.

So, within fifteen minutes, I was in the office and the next thing I know I was getting searched and caught with all my vegetables (pot). This is such a memorable experience for me because getting caught was the beginning of the end for me. Later I would get in a collision of havoc and bad luck and you catching me was the beginning of a three month streak of being terrible unlucky. You also helped me get kicked out of BHS and sent to Penn. All of these things mentioned were all bad during the time, but now I've been erased and rewritten, and best of all will be walking across the stage laughing all the way home. So thanks.

Jesse Arnold

Letters like this give me the courage to stand strong, to know that getting a kid in trouble at the right time might very well be the crucial difference in helping that student wake up to the error of his or her ways. I love Jesse's line near the end when he says he has been "erased and rewritten." Aren't we all—as people, as students, as teachers—a rough draft, one needing constant revision as we slowly come to better understand who we are and what we are trying to say with our life. This reminds me of a wonderful poem, "Ask Me," by William Stafford:

> Some time when the river is ice ask me
> mistakes I have made. Ask me whether
> what I have done is my life. Others
> have come in their slow way into
> my thought, and some have tried to help
> or to hurt: ask me what difference
> their strongest love or hate has made. I will listen to what you say.
> You and I can turn and look
> at the silent river and wait. We know

the current is there, hidden; and there
are comings and goings from miles away
that hold the stillness exactly before us.
What the river says, that is what I say.[2]

Stafford reminds me of the importance of error, the blessings of failure. When asked one time about his writing process, Stafford said he got up every morning, made tea, and sat on the couch in his front room, writing about whatever came to him. He forced himself to write every morning. When the interviewer asked him about the quality of such a process, if he ever wrote bad poems, Stafford simply said that many were terrible. "What do you do when you write such bad poems?" the interviewer asked. "I just lower my standards, of course, so I can consider it a successful morning," he replied, because the point is to keep at it, to move through the bad stuff in order to find the good stuff.

This may be important for you to remember in the next two weeks as the first round of grades go out. Grades are a troublesome aspect of our work and can, at least for periods of time, complicate our relationship with students. The kid who loves you but gets in trouble at home for a D or C (did I neglect to mention the F?) is not always willing to accept responsibility for that grade and so will sometimes turn and direct their frustration at you, as if the grade is somehow a reflection on them as a person or your regard for them. "How could she give me a D if she really liked me?" the student wants to scream. But it is in the shadow of such a moment, when those grades go out and the student must confront themselves with the consequences of their decisions, that you can often reach and convert a few new kids. Not all, but a few. This is a one-kid-at-a-time kind of business. So be ready to help those kids rise to the challenge in the weeks ahead, to let them know you honor them by expecting more and are willing to help them meet your high standards. As I tell my kids sometimes, "No one ever comes back when they are twenty-five and says, 'Hey, Mr. Burke, thanks for expecting so little of me. It really paid off.'"

You know you are expecting just the right amount when everyone is complaining a bit about the work; it's like the body when it aches because you used new muscles, you strained them. Weight lifters know that in order to build new muscle, you have to actually tear the muscles a bit and help them heal and thereby improve or strengthen themselves. I needed to remember this last week when many kids in my AP English class were complaining—pretty much all of them, actually. But when I reflected on their complaints, I realized they were struggling because it was new; the assignment got them outside of their comfort zone and forced them to think in ways they had not before, to do what they had not done before, or at least not at this level. This had the effect of inspiring in them, once they got over their frustration, a new level of commitment that began to gel by the week's end. They wanted me to do their work, but that would have resulted only in *me* learning, not the students.[3] My thoughts on this can be summed up through the words of a principal who I once heard describing his school's philosophy: "I place the kids in the midst of manageable difficulty and help them work through the demands of the assignment on their own." At the end of class yesterday you may have heard me asking the kids for feedback on the process, asking them to write down on an index card what was hard and what helped; in this way they come to learn more about their own process, to learn about themselves as learners.

I want to end with a page that summarizes some of my thoughts in a slightly more formal way. In my book *School Smarts: The Four Cs of Academic Success*, I tried to answer the question, "Who succeeds in school and why?" Throughout this letter today, whether stated or implied, the concept of commitment (the first of the Four Cs) appears.[4] I think these Four Cs explain your own success this year, too, for they apply just as much to us as to the kids. Certainly they help me understand what I have to do and why my efforts are paying off in the AP English class. I read and worked constantly on the AP course from the moment I knew I would teach it back in April. Much of what I did was fill myself up with new knowledge and ideas (content), upgrade and reflect on the skills I would need if I was to be effective (competencies), and concentrate on improving my own speed, stamina (those AP books are *so* long, so fat, so thick!), and capacity to see connections, patterns, and so on (capacity). I hope you find the Four Cs model useful, not only as it applies to your students but also as it applies to you. I am also including a copy of the lesson plan template I'm using (it evolves as I do) this year to design my lessons (see Figure 14.1). You will note that it has not only the Four Cs but a few other things of possible interest. The Academic Essentials mentioned on the lesson plan template are on the other page I have enclosed. These, too, are evolving, but in their latest incarnation they offer me a useful guide.

I should end by telling you how much I appreciate the opportunity to write these letters. I always learn so much about my own teaching by writing about it. These letters are special in that they are a much more private, ongoing dialogue—not just with you but with myself—about this work we both love so much. I can only hope you are finding them as helpful as I do, for to talk about what you should do reminds me of what *I* should do. In this way, we are left with the ultimate realization that we are always learning, are always students, even when we have become teachers of not only our students but ourselves.

Enjoy the week ahead.

Your colleague,

Jim

Question 6

What is your approach to teaching writing?

⟿

Dear Joy:

I have been reading papers for hours and thought, by way of a break, I would allow myself a little time to begin my answer to your important question about writing. Based on what I've been reading the last few hours, one would think my "approach" was to create in students' minds a great storm of confusion and ask them to capture that in a series of increasingly abstract, convoluted, and often terrible sentences. I have learned to trust the process, though, to see in their struggles the beginning of learning; that is, so long as I know how to lead them through it and they trust me to do so.

Thus to speak of writing is to speak of teaching and of *learning*. I find it useful to consider students' performance in light of a continuum (see Figure 6.1).[1]

Consider juggling as a simple example of the process by which we learn: the novice begins with one ball and two hands. They achieve immediate and complete mastery! As soon as you complicate the task by adding a second object to juggle or *a new way* to juggle the lone ball, errors increase, as does frustration. This is where my seniors are now with writing: they must juggle not only more demands (tossed to them by the College Board) but more objects, handling not just the single literary text but three or four, and applying to these texts others' ideas about tragedy (Aristotle, Arthur Miller, et al.). Thus their writing sounds like breaking fishbowls and splatting tomatoes, reads like colliding chainsaws and terrified goldfish. And this is exactly where I want them to be, for these are the conditions for growth. I have created in them a series of problems I must now teach them how to solve on their own. I have a context for my teaching, as they do for their learning. To the extent that my lessons help them solve these problems, help them juggle these demands with grace and confidence, the students will commit themselves and do what I ask. I must, however, create some sense of what Mike Schmoker (in his fine little book *Results*) calls "rapid results."[2]

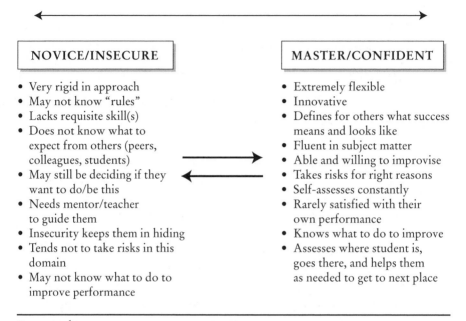

CONTINUUM OF PERFORMANCE
(as a reader, writer, thinker, teacher, speaker, etc.)

NOVICE/INSECURE

- Very rigid in approach
- May not know "rules"
- Lacks requisite skill(s)
- Does not know what to expect from others (peers, colleagues, students)
- May still be deciding if they want to do/be this
- Needs mentor/teacher to guide them
- Insecurity keeps them in hiding
- Tends not to take risks in this domain
- May not know what to do to improve performance

MASTER/CONFIDENT

- Extremely flexible
- Innovative
- Defines for others what success means and looks like
- Fluent in subject matter
- Able and willing to improvise
- Takes risks for right reasons
- Self-assesses constantly
- Rarely satisfied with their own performance
- Knows what to do to improve
- Assesses where student is, goes there, and helps them as needed to get to next place

FIGURE 6.1[1]

There is a misguided notion that students must just write, write, write—and they will learn, improve. There is a difference, however, between just writing and actually *practicing*, for when we practice, we are intentional. As a highly ranked tennis player in my teens, I never just played: I practiced my topspin backhand down the line, my crosscourt slice, my American twist second serve, concentrating each time on some aspect of placement, always refining my control. So it goes, I believe, with writing: kids must learn it as a craft, one they can hone, perfect through guided instruction, modeling, and individual coaching in the form of comments at their desks or in the margins.

But as these last two days have reminded me all too well, we work within constraints that keep us forever stranded between what we *should* do and what we *can* do, given the time and the number of students we have. When I mentioned the demands of teaching writing and of responding to writing on a listserv I run for teachers,[3] Leif Fearn, coauthor of *Interactions: Teaching Writing and the Language Arts*, wrote:

Regarding the reading load, there is an incontrovertible truth: "If they write as much as they must in order to learn to write well, I cannot possibly read it all; if they write as much as I can read, they cannot possibly learn to write well." Begin there.

> *Question*: When they write a three-page paper is the third page better written than the second, the second than the first?
>
> *Question*: When they write a three-page paper, or a five, have they three, or five, pages of worthy material?
>
> *Question*: Do young writers who do not write very well write better when they write 3-, 4-, or 5-page papers than they do when they write 1- or 2-page papers?
>
> *Question*: When young writers have to introduce an argument, and conclude from it, do they need more than one page, more than a half-page? Can an argument be introduced in a sentence, posed and explained in two or three, and concluded in one?

> Most effective writers tell us that brevity is the key to precision.
>
> Teach them to think in and write sentences, perhaps even elegant ones on occasion. Can anyone name a resource that shows teachers how to teach young writers to think in and write sentences, perhaps even elegant ones? No, not to describe sentences or to define them, parse or combine them; rather, to think in and write them.
>
> Questions, always questions. [4]

Carol Jago, author of *Cohesive Writing*, responded to my question with this:

> As a teacher who brought home 114 (not that I'm counting) student papers to read this weekend, the issue is foremost in my mind.
>
> I think the most valuable advice I can offer is something I learned from Peter Elbow. Respond like a reader. When students feel that we are trying to follow their argument, they seem to be able to hear our criticism more clearly.
>
> For example:
>
> - Use questions ("How does this follow from your thesis?" rather than "Incoherent")
> - Let the student know when you are lost (never write "awk")
> - Include the student's name in your notes

Donald Graves says that writing teachers should be doctors, not judges. Works for me. [5]

Finally, on the subject of responding to writing, I surveyed two classes of AP English students who are all seniors and want to write well (or think they already do). Their comments came minutes after getting a paper back, their first real paper of the year.[6] Most of them see themselves as good writers; I see them as people with a range of skills, all of whom have a lot to learn. Now I have to confess, I did a lousy job with these papers. Not because I just slapped a grade on them and handed them back, but because I didn't know what I was trying to achieve through this paper. So instead of marking a few things related to what I have been teaching (as I would usually do), I tended to overcompensate and mark everything, but not even in a useful way. This led to my question to the kids: What kind of response from teachers do you find most helpful as a writer?

Some made general comments about what helps: Tell us what we did wrong so we can avoid it, but also what we did well so we can keep doing it. Others were more severe: "I like to hear what I did to deserve the grade, not the good things. I already know them. What I need to know is what I'm missing or what I did wrong. We don't need ego-boosters." Duncan, of course, is applying to Stanford and so is a bit more thick-skinned and practical than kids in a sophomore class like you are teaching. Others said they get overwhelmed and depressed if the teacher marks all their mistakes; they find it more helpful if we just focus on one or two things. Many stressed how much they prefer to talk over their paper since the discussion is more responsive to their individual needs. This is, naturally, the most effective and thus impossible to do: How can I have great writing conferences with thirty-five kids? I can't. So what do I do? I use peer response groups, giving them specific tasks and guidelines to follow. I might say, for instance, that I want them only to ask questions about things that are not clear to them as they read. In fact, this is one of the strategies some kids found most useful: to ask questions of their writing like "What are you trying to say here?" or "How does this relate to the main idea of the paragraph?"

Writing is among the most personal aspects of their learning, for it is the most public performance of our intelligence. Those mistakes, some of which can be embarrassing, hang out like dirty laundry for all the world to see, so some students try to avoid writing. They develop an identity of themselves as a "terrible writer" or someone who "just can't write." This is why I find the Four Cs useful: it allows me to understand that students might not show the commitment (C^1) because they lack the necessary content knowledge (C^2) and competencies (C^3) or simply don't possess the requisite capacities (C^4) such as speed and stamina. I myself did not realize how much there was to know about writing until I stumbled into a graduate program on the teaching of writing while getting my teaching credential. I had an entire course in the sentence—for a whole semester! I admit that it was my infatuation with the teacher that initially inspired me to work so hard (going into Rosemary's office for extra help as often as possible—I mean, when I needed help); however, it was the beauty of the sentence and an emerging love of language and craft that carried me through the rest of the course and, ultimately, the program.

From that program came an understanding of not just how writing works but how writers work. People must have something to say, something they care about, if they are to write well, to feel a sense of ownership, to take any pride in what they write. Otherwise it is just an assignment. Thus another aspect of my approach is to always do my best to give kids some room to choose when it comes to what they write about. I don't always have the option to let them—or believe they always should—choose *how* they write; chances are I am trying to teach them persuasive writing, for example, even though they want to write a story or a poem. Nor does this worry me, because I think writing adds discipline to their thinking, makes them realize how language works, and gives them a sense of accomplishment when they do write something well, for they know how much work they had to put into it to make it shine.

We can't just send kids off to write on their own, however, and expect brilliant work. Here we must be like masters guiding the apprentice through the work, using techniques and tools (e.g., graphic organizers) to help them generate possible topics, evaluate and choose from these the best one, which they must then think about until they can craft a good thesis. This is a complicated part of the process for many kids, even in the most advanced classes, for they suddenly get anxious, worrying that they do not have anything to say, that they are not, in fact, as smart as they thought they were.

One writing assignment captures most of what I believe is important when it comes to writing: the Weekly Paper.[7] I created a "digital textbook" for the class; this was a website with texts in many formats and genres: from paintings to videos, poems to primary source documents, histories of words to speeches of world leaders. It was literary and political, scientific and artistic, contemporary and classical. We revised it as we went, adding new links as we found them, taking off old ones we found useless. After listening to a Kitchen Sisters audio diary, or reading about the life of Picasso, watching a video from *Americans' Favorite Poems*, or reading the Gettysburg Address at the Library of Congress website, they had to write a great one-page paper.

This assignment improved their writing and created a sustainable context in which to effectively teach writing. They had to write one page of polished writing a week. They could choose the medium, the subject, the stance, the voice. But I could also make choices about what to teach based on what their writing revealed. If they lacked a variety of sentence types, or tended (as a group) to use weak or passive verbs, I could put their single pages up on the overhead and talk about it out loud, celebrating what worked and helping them understand what didn't and then showing them how to fix it. This created a cycle of submission and response that resulted in substantial improvement, which inspired in them greater commitment to their writing. I think this improvement and commitment were due not only to the choice of topic and type of text but also to the scope of the assignment: it seemed reasonable, doable, and resulted in an improvement they could feel.

By way of contrast, let me show you something I did in the last few days—something that demanded a lot from me but helped me realize what my advanced writers need. One girl in the AP class wrote the following in response to my question about what kind of feedback helps:

> I feel that the feedback I received was not very helpful. I always read what you write, and I usually agree, however where you wrote that my paragraph about "Dan White" being "misplaced," I disagree. It should be reevaluated. That paragraph supports my claim. I spent a significant amount of time on this paper, and I would appreciate a re-evaluation for a better understanding of why I got a score of six.

I accepted Mara's invitation to think more deeply about her writing. I didn't care about her grade; in fact, the longer I studied her essay the more I wondered why I even gave it a six! But I needed to understand what was going on with her as a person and a writer. So I emailed Mara that night:

> Hi Mara:
>
> I've been sitting here, reading through the feedback cards from class today. Things are never very neat and too productive in the rush of the end of class. I left our conversation today dissatisfied with our exchange. I just want you to know that I listened to you, and that I respect your commitment to your growth as a writer. Writing is a strange, complex craft that takes time to learn; it doesn't help, to be honest, when the whole grading thing is added to the process. That distracts from the real mess of learning to write well. What I want you to realize about your essay, which we can discuss next week if you'd like, is that there is a difference between

the purpose something serves and whether it effectively achieves that goal. On the card, which I appreciated you taking time to write, you said that you disagreed with me because "it supports your thesis." I want you by year's end not just to be able to support your thesis with the best examples, but to write in polished, brilliant prose that will make you proud and your readers tremble . . . or sigh . . . or just say, Wow.

I've worked for about four hours today just studying students' remarks and a bunch of books. I tell you this because getting better, learning what we need if we are to do our work well, takes time and effort, two things I know you are willing to invest in your own growth as a writer. I know it can be hard to have someone reject or otherwise not appreciate some aspect of your writing. I've also learned to humble myself and just listen to what others say about my writing (and my teaching). Ultimately, writing is not about whether the writer likes or understands it but whether the *reader* understands what the writer says and responds as the writer intended. So you're welcome to disagree with me, but in my experience you will learn a lot more if you find a way to learn from what your readers say, especially when you are in the midst of learning how to do something better.

I came into the class already respecting you for your work ethic: I watched you come into Mrs. McClain's class all last year to prepare your presentations and clarify assignments. You're a model student and I want you to leave my class in June glad of the time we spent together and with your hands full of what I was able to teach you. Perhaps with future writing assignments we can work together a bit more on the front side of the assignment, meeting at lunch to go over it; or you can send me portions to respond to via email when you aren't sure if something works.

A rather long response for a Friday night. Take this letter, if nothing else, as evidence of my commitment to you and your success. Thanks for your comments today; they taught me important things.

See you Monday.

Mr. Burke

I had no idea how she would respond, especially since she was challenging my authority and credibility in her original note. She wrote back the next day:

Dear Mr. Burke:

I want to thank you so much for your response. I greatly appreciate the fact that you spent time contemplating my questions and concerns about my paper. That means a lot to me as a student. It shows that you care and

I think it is important for a student to establish a connection with a teacher. Thanks.

I want you to know that this was one of the few times that I have questioned a grade. I am, and always have been, open to constructive criticism. However in this case, I believe that a misunderstanding has taken place. Being new in your class, it has not yet been made clear to me what the current criteria for a writing style would be. Absent your interpretation of those guidelines, my only choice is to write clearly and logically, which I feel I have achieved in this paper. Is creative style more important than clearly supported ideas at the AP level?

I understand that we as students are supposed to look at AP English as a "college level course," and I am looking forward to grow to this level. For college level writing I do have a few questions. For example, what should each paragraph contain? How should I intertwine ideas? Should the ideas be sequential? It would be helpful to go over these points for each essay topic. I do want to develop as a writer, but without knowing what specifically is required, my evaluation can only be based on a trial and error effort.

Your dedication as a teacher is inspirational. I will do my best to comply with what you require from me as a writer and student and thanks again.

Mara Soss

What intrigues me about students like Mara is their desire to succeed as a student so that they might succeed as a person in the world for which we are all helping them prepare. For writing at its core is about deciding what to say and how to say it, who you are and what you believe; all of this is reflected in the language we use to express ourselves. Taken a step further, we might see our students not as students, but authors, people responsible for writing the story their life will tell through the choices they make. We need, all of us, the chance to revise ourselves, to move through the seasons of error, the lack of clarity and cohesion that follows us around at points in our life, until we come to the hands of a teacher who can, through their gifts, help us find our voice, the one that is really ours, that has waited for us to find and claim it. Then we can—as I do to Mace Perona, Ken Kitchener, Rosemary Patton, Catherine Lucas, and Bill Robinson—turn and say thank you with the grace they invested in us through their love of language and, in a way, of us, for what is teaching if not an act of love for all that we might do for the world that is ours.

After all, long ago, the same person who writes you this letter and all the others wrote this poem:

> I'm calling for affection
> Avoiding neglection
> It scares me so
> To find myself alone
> I can't think of
> Any worse fear than living without love
> No matter what the price
> Please take my advice
> Find someone soon, one who'll provide protection
> And answer your call for affection.

Neglection? That's me at sixteen, the age of all those kids in your fourth-period class. I was Holden and Huck, spending my days at the river of my youth, waiting for I knew not what, for I did not yet realize that my life was my story to write. For now, though, your class is the story you are writing, and you are writing it well, and each of your kids is grateful to be a character in that story.

Your colleague,

Jim

Interlude 2

AN EMAIL EXCHANGE: YOU SEEM DISCOURAGED . . .

Dear Joy:

When I saw you this morning you seemed discouraged. You hang in there, now. You seemed a bit unsure of yourself today. You do your work, do it the best you can at that time, on that day, and move on, committed to doing better next time. The mistakes I make on a typical day this year in my AP classes, which I have never taught before, would number more than the stars, and it matters not that few see them but me, for I see them as brightly as the stars outside my window tonight. But just as I do not let them define me, nor should you. Boston Symphony conductor Benjamin Zander[1] teaches his musicians to raise their hands and proclaim, "How fascinating!" when they mess up, seeing in it a chance to better understand the complexity of the music. Keep your faith in all its forms and let it keep you strong during the all the seasons of your work, but never doubt that you are a teacher and always remember that your students are lucky to have you. Everyone knows that sophomores are the toughest class to teach.

Jim

~ ~

Jim,

Thanks for your email. I *just* received it. You identified my condition correctly. It just is so hard! There is always an endless list of things "I should" be teaching them and there never seems enough time to teach it all (partly because transition between areas seems difficult for many of them—which I am trying to work on to shorten these times for fourth period). In addition, I feel I miserably fail to produce the wonder and curiosity I long for them to have (I want to be like John Steinbeck's teacher who imparted the wonder and curiosity to her students). No, my class is not running amok, but they just aren't "with me" right now. And at present I am forced to toughen up my stance concerning behavioral issues. There is tension in my class; things aren't jelling like I want them to. Trying to intrigue them about a topic seems nearly impossible. And so it is difficult. Of course I am too hard on myself (which is good and bad at the same time). But . . .

I was reminded on Sunday about what perseverance is: one who remains faithful under difficult circumstances. I must remain faithful to my passionate commitment to teaching students and just pray that amidst the struggle and tension my students will see my love for them and for literature and then think/live differently. Thank you for your affirmation; it is often the boost I need to reaffirm myself and calm the current storm inside me about teaching.

See you tomorrow.

Joy

> *My students seem to be bored out of their minds. How can*
> *I possibly compete with lunch, the weekend, and all their*
> *other interests? I feel like I am inflicting them with Chinese*
> *water torture or something. What can I do?*

Dear Joy:

Good work, that is, work that means something, that makes a difference, that earns the respect of others, is inevitably *hard* work. Its complexity takes time to master, even to realize sometimes, for the true master too often makes the work appear much easier than it really is. Inherent in such important work is struggle, humiliation, and inevitable pain, which is why we feel such pride and satisfaction when our work goes well. We alone know the price we paid for that one minute of seamless learning, those five minutes of flawless teaching, those thirty minutes of engaged discussion, which we know we must earn again the next day, returning each day as if we were a beginner all over again.[1]

This might not be what you want to hear right now. I'm sure you'd rather I list out a few nickels of knowledge you can plug and play so that you can feel like the professional, the master you want to become. But that is not what I have to tell you, nor is it what you need to hear. You need to know that every great—and I mean *great*—teacher I know tried to quit at some point, felt they were a fraud or a failure. I have the resignation letter from one woman who told her principal she had no business being a teacher; she went on—after he refused to accept her resignation—to become not only a master teacher but the head of her department, a mentor to decades of excellent teachers (all of whom remember her with the greatest respect), and the leader of a national educational organization that shaped policy and curriculum for millions of kids across the country. When she retired last year, hundreds celebrated her, people from all areas of her work, all of whom learned from her, from a woman so much like yourself in spirit and potential, a woman who at about the same point in her career as you said she had no business being a teacher.

I recently watched *Comedian*, a documentary about Jerry Seinfeld and his return to stand-up comedy. (Bear with me: it's related, I promise.) After

Seinfeld stopped doing his television show, he decided to return to his roots: stand-up. What's more, he decided to retire all his old material and create a whole new act. The film documents his efforts—and serious struggles—to create a new act from scratch. Throughout the documentary are interviews with other comedians, the masters of American comedy, all of whom say the same thing: he's crazy to get rid of his material, to start over. The documentary is brutal and honest about the difficulty of the comedian's craft. You see Jerry Seinfeld standing on stage staring into the lights as some joke fades from his memory—or just doesn't work—halfway through telling it; then you see him reach into his back pocket, a look of despair crossing his face as he stands there reading over his notes for the joke, looking like me when my lesson plan stalls, consulting the map of my lesson as I try to find my way back. You see Seinfeld just stalling, and finally giving up and going home, shaking his head, wondering how he ever made it as a comedian in the first place. In one of the scenes, Seinfeld and Chris Rock talk about how much material Seinfeld has assembled for the new act. "I have fifteen minutes of good material after *four* months," he tells Rock, who immediately responds with evident respect and even surprise, saying how remarkable that is. All I could think was: *"Fifteen minutes! In four months?"* And then: "Teachers have to go in *five* days a week and do *five* shows a day for *fifty-five* minutes!" If Barry Bonds goes up to bat five times in a game, he will likely strike out twice, get walked, *maybe* single, and probably homer *once*. And they consider him one of the greats. There are no performance-enhancing drugs for teachers; there is only the steady work of the master, carefully attaching what might to what does work and then shaving off what does not fit, to eventually produce what is worthy of their name.

When your email came through, I had just finished the short reflection I write in my *Teacher's Daybook* every Friday.[2] Here is what I wrote this week:

> We will all—and always—make mistakes; the only question is whether we learn from them. Everything I did this week in the AP class is or feels like 1.0; so when it doesn't work or work well, I can only say that I thought it would, then study why it didn't or, if it's viable, make the necessary adjustments and try again, but differently. I think the important thing is that I learned a lot about what doesn't work, and glimpsed a few things that do, so I can go into the weekend saying I did good work that I know I can improve.

As I said, you may want solutions, methods that can mend your despair. And I want you to find them, but I don't want to mislead you as to where those solutions lie. They lie not only inside yourself but in the books of the masters, which you must read, and the classrooms of the masters (like Diane McClain and Elaine Caret), which you must visit and observe as you figure out what kind of teacher you want to be, what your identity as a teacher is. You see in yourself a failure when you are "forced to be stern" or "change your focus," but I hear in that an emerging persona and mastery as you learn to rule, to lead—to *teach*. And when you go to your sixth period at Mills and have the courage to ask them why they enjoy other classes, you show that you are "made of sterner stuff" and are committed to completing the journey you have begun. It's possible that teaching public-school English in this era is the most difficult work there is; surely there is nothing *more* difficult or more trying. To paraphrase the poet Louise Gluck, what resists us shapes us.

You worry about "competing with lunch or brunch or the weekend," but let me put you at ease: you are competing only against yourself, trying to do better today than you did yesterday, trying to do better in fifth period than you did in fourth with the same material. If I bomb second period and manage four minutes and twenty-three seconds of engaged discussion about the same text in third period, I go home content with the knowledge that there is something there to work with, something to improve. I once heard the poet Philip Levine say he had made kids at the best colleges around the country cry; this seemed an odd claim to make while speaking about the exacting demands of the poet's craft. He said that when he told kids at Harvard that they had three good lines in their thirty-line poem, they often broke down and cried; they were used to being told their work was brilliant. And so they turned away from it, avoided what was difficult. At Fresno State, however, hardly a university where one would expect to find one of the nation's greatest living poets, Levine said the students were different. If he told kids they had three great lines and rest was junk, they were thrilled because their three good lines told them they could improve, they had something to work with. So it is with teaching, a craft made of moments we weave into a larger fabric called a lesson, a unit, a class. Such work, especially if one wants to achieve a sense of mastery, demands discipline and resiliency, patience and humility, courage and conviction.

Of all the poems that mean so much to me, it is Jack Gilbert's poem "The Abnormal Is Not Courage" that keeps me honest about the demands of our work. Here is the poem:

The Poles rode out from Warsaw against the German
Tanks on horses. Rode knowing, in sunlight, with sabers,
A magnitude of beauty that allows me no peace.
And yet this poem would lessen that day. Question
The bravery. Say it's not courage. Call it a passion.
Would say courage isn't that. Not at its best.
It was impossible, and with form. They rode in sunlight,
Were mangled. But I say courage is not the abnormal.
Not the marvelous act. Not Macbeth with fine speeches.
The worthless can manage in public, or for the moment.
It is too near the whore's heart: the bounty of impulse,
And the failure to sustain even small kindness.
Not the marvelous act, but the evident conclusion of being.
Not strangeness, but a leap forward of the same quality.
Accomplishment. The even loyalty. But fresh.
Not the Prodigal Son, nor Faustus. But Penelope.
The thing steady and clear. Then the crescendo.
The real form. The culmination. And the exceeding.
Not the surprise. The amazed understanding. The marriage,
Not the month's rapture. Not the exception. The beauty
That is of many days. Steady and clear.
It is the normal excellence, of long accomplishment.[3]

It is in the last third of this magnificent poem that I find strength and wisdom. We want to go in each day and teach like Jaime Escalante, like all the inspired teachers we have ever seen in the movies. But that's not the world you and I live in, Joy. My week was made not of "marvelous acts" or "surprises," but of moments so small most did not notice them: Nick saying he suddenly understood how hard it was to write a great sentence, Marina raising her hand for the first time, a boy finishing his first book ever, a boy asking if he could sit down over lunch and discuss how he might improve his essay. I'm forty-two, twice your age; it took me all these years to learn how to talk to that boy about his paper, to learn how to create the conditions necessary for that girl to raise her hand, to understand how a sentence works and how to get kids to see it, too. I bought that knowledge of craft through the long hours of study that lie ahead of you, which begin with the anger and frustration, even despair, that you feel now, and led you to choose teaching, to embrace the problems you will spend your whole life seeking to solve. On some days, you'll feel like you have solved them, only to find upon your return the next day that your solutions don't apply any-more because the problems have changed somehow. But your knowledge stays with you, making it easier to find the solutions each time, and in this way you get more fluent, more efficient, more effective; I'm not sure that our work ever becomes easier, though, because we seem always to be trying to accomplish more.

There seems to be a movement afoot that implies one needn't know anything to be an effective teacher so long as you have an adult present to "deliver" the curriculum, but this defies what the reliable research consis-tently shows: the knowledge and skill of the teacher make the most signifi-cant and consistent difference. That continuum I included in a previous letter[4] applies just as much to you or me as to your students; we are always moving back and forth along it as we teach new materials or try new tech-niques, teach new classes or move to new schools. Too often we get snared in an either-or kind of thinking that implies we either are or are not, should or should not be a teacher; give yourself time to learn, to be less than perfect, to make the inevitable mistakes from which you will learn. The old skiers' adage is true: If you aren't falling down, you aren't trying hard enough.

This has been a hard letter to write, Joy, and perhaps a hard letter to read. But I think it's important for you to understand the nature of our work; oth-erwise the difficulties, the failures will seem to emanate from you, from some flaw or aspect of yourself. When I was about to leave for Tunisia to teach in the Peace Corps, my principal told me that the work would be hard, would make me feel like quitting at times. Everyone knows it is hard. He told me to stay there, to stick it out no matter how hard it got. This was strangely reassuring, for when things got hard, it confirmed what I had been told and freed me up from thinking that it was my fault, that I was inade-quate. I didn't know it then, but I was storing up strength and courage, both of which I would need when I returned home to become a teacher.

For now, you have done what I know makes the biggest difference: You asked your students what helps, what they need. You asked a colleague (me) for guidance, for reassurance that it is supposed to be as hard as it is. And you pulled back to reflect on what you are doing and why and how you might improve so that you can be the teacher you dream of being. I see you work every day and know your gifts. You are like John Lennon, who, when asked if he ever listened to his own albums, said that he never did, for he could hear only the mistakes and think of all the things he *should* have done.

I am grateful for the chance you give me, through our letters, to think about our work and come to better understand it myself. I never watch you teach without thinking how good you are and how much better you will become if you have faith in yourself and the process through which we revise ourselves if we find the courage you continue to show.

Your colleague,

Jim

P.S.: I do have more practical things I want to share with you, but this was the letter I needed to write for now because it seemed to me this is what you wanted to hear. I will follow up with a letter that focuses on some more specific classroom management issues, which I realize are urgent issues for you. In the meantime, I am attaching an article I clipped for you from a recent professional journal (see Appendix A).[5]

⌒

Dear Joy:

I began as a poet. This is how language first came to me. A few letters back, I included some embarrassing scrap I wrote in high school, but for years really, I focused on writing nothing but poetry. When I left to work in Tunisia, in the Peace Corps, a poetic mentor gave me a packet of poems whose authors have kept me company ever since, though of course I have added to the list. Certain poets, however, remain so vital that they are more like my personal saints, my guides, the Dantes (or, rather, the Virgils) who lead me through the labyrinth of this life, keeping me company through their words. Who are these poets, these personal companions? Jack Gilbert, Czeslaw Milosz, Kenneth Rexroth, William Stafford, Seamus Heaney, Rainer Maria Rilke, Mary Oliver, and Philip Levine. Other poets matter, are also essential voices in the choir: Sharon Olds, Marge Piercy, William Carlos Williams, Lucille Clifton, Li-Young Lee.

My relationship with poetry changed dramatically as the demands of teaching and family intensified. After years of immersing myself in novels, I realized that poetry offered the most viable opportunity to keep reading despite the many demands of my work. There was always time for a poem, a haiku if nothing else. So I began keeping a book of poems with me at all times; put another by the coffee machine; piled a few in the bathroom; propped up a couple next to my computer to read between assignments or while a long document was printing. These early efforts led me to use more poetry in my classes, often not as any part of a formal unit, but instead as a gift, an offering with no other purpose than to engage, to challenge, to share, to make us think as we began class or entered into a discussion. I often take a small anthology with me to the copy room when I go; that way

I can read a poem or two if I have to wait. It sometimes happens that while reading these poems, I find one that grabs me and demands to be shared. So I will walk into the class and just share it, saying nothing more than, "I thought this was incredible and had to share it with you."

Several things come out of such encounters. First, my kids continually see that I actually read what I assign, that, as a kid said once, "Mr. Burke actually thinks this stuff is important." So there is a professional benefit insofar as reading poetry (or anything else I share with or refer to while teaching my kids) enhances my credibility. Too many teachers claim they have no time to read, but isn't reading why we entered the field, took those classes in the first place? If we don't read for ourselves, our roots will wither and decay and eventually bring us down like the trees in the front of school that periodically fall after the roots grow weak. Diane McClain, for example, *always* has a book going for her own pleasure, and not some cheap thriller either. It's what keeps her alive, what keeps her such an energized teacher; it's what keeps her from resenting teaching and all its demands; it's what makes her *an interesting person*. If we let our teaching keep us from what we love, we will grow to resent and ultimately hate it. It doesn't matter how much you read, but that you *do*: sometimes I will sit down to work at 7:21 P.M. and say to myself, "OK, you can read from Tracy Kidder's *Mountains Beyond Mountains* (my current personal book that I just *have* to read from) until 7:30." Then when I begin grading papers or preparing lessons at 7:30, I feel good about things. Later on, at 9:48, having read papers or school-related literature for a few hours, I will say, "OK, you can take a break until 10:00 and read a couple poems from that new Philip Levine book (*Breath*) while you make some hot chocolate or popcorn."

Another benefit to bringing poetry into the classroom: cross-germination of texts. What do you get when you mix a William Stafford poem (like "Fifteen") with *Catcher in the Rye*? A great class, a rich discussion, and good thinking that ensures that students do some real work. You can also read poems many times, a benefit that is often overlooked but has great value when teaching kids to read closely. They can read it for different reasons each time, focusing now on content, now on imagery, later on connections to another book or associations with themes in other poems we have read. Such encounters make the classroom a minefield of potentially dangerous (in the good sense) moments during which the readers face themselves or some other truth. I've included a few pages from one of my favorite books about teaching; in this excerpt from *Tuned in and Fired Up*, Sam Intrator shows how a teacher uses poetry to kindle a powerful conversation within the classroom and inside the minds of the kids in the class.[1]

I bring poems into the classroom by different routes, for different purposes. What I *don't* do (though it's not to say it can't be done effectively) is a one-hit-wonder *big poetry unit*. Instead, while reading *Lord of the Flies* or *Catcher in the Rye*, I will weave a collection of poems throughout the unit. It's worth noting that the word *poet* means "maker" or "creator"; moreover, the word *text* stems from the notion of weaving, as in *text*ile. Thus I see the class as a text itself that we, as poet-teachers, must weave through the choices we make. Just as the actual weaver considers texture, color, and style when creating something, so must we consider text type, themes, subject, and so on when stitching together our class. For *Catcher in the Rye*, for instance, you might consider looking at Naomi Shihab Nye's anthology *What Have You Lost?* which I have in the room and you are welcome to borrow.[2]

In addition to integrating a collection of different poems into the unit, I also have students study one poet in depth each year, choosing a different poem from their collected works each week (or as often as possible). When I last taught sophomores, we read Yusef Konumyakaa, a powerful African American poet who writes about a range of subjects. His poems are accessible but challenging, familiar yet foreign at the same time. Another valuable aspect of his poetry is that you can find excellent audio recordings of him reading them on various Internet sites. So kids can read it aloud, hear him read it with perhaps a different emphasis, and then reread it as many times as they wish till they feel they understand it well. A poem like "The Deck," which I am including for you to read, is just one example of his talent.[3]

I typically choose an author whose work I really like so I *have* to spend all that time reading from their books. It's also essential that the poet be one whose work the kids will appreciate, though perhaps not at first. It is important that the poet's work be accessible, but not obvious. And the poet must have written enough that we can follow them over their career and see how they have changed, how their style or subject matter has evolved. Other poets I have tried or considered: Seamus Heaney, Langston Hughes, Sharon Olds, Li-Young Lee, Gary Soto (and this year, in my AP class, John Donne and Wallace Stevens).

This is all about poetry for the professional side of our lives, though: poems to bake up and serve to the kids. I want to return to the role of poetry in my own life, the poetry that sustains me as a teacher *and a person*. Our work is filled with moments of doubt, times late at night (for me, anyway) when we feel lost. At such moments I turn to someone like William Stafford for a poem like this:

> THE WAY IT IS
>
> There's a thread you follow. It goes among
> things that change. But it doesn't change.
> People wonder about what you are pursuing.
> You have to explain about the thread.
> But it is hard for others to see.
> While you hold it you can't get lost.
> Tragedies happen; people get hurt
> or die; and you suffer and get old.
> Nothing you do can stop time's unfolding.
> You don't ever let go of that thread.[4]

It is not always clear to others, or even to ourselves, for that matter, what we are "pursuing." Poems like this renew my faith, teach me to follow what I know is right even if don't yet know its name. I am enclosing for you a copy of the book I turn to most often, for it is in *Teaching with Fire: Poetry That Sustains the Courage to Teach* that you will find not only these poems but wonderful brief meditations from teachers about how these poems help them, about the role poetry plays in their personal and professional lives.[5]

My faith and interest in poetry have given me several opportunities for rich personal *and* professional renewal that I want to tell you about before I close. Every year the National Endowment for the Humanities (NEH) offers summer institutes all over the country (some even go to other countries such as England and France) for studying authors and subjects.[6] The Faulkner seminar in Mississippi, for example, is a rare opportunity to study Faulkner for six weeks under the guidance of a major Faulkner scholar. I have done two, both related to poetry: a summer in Wisconsin studying the book of Psalms as poetry and an institute in Amherst, Massachusetts, studying John Berryman and William Carlos Williams under Paul Mariani, who wrote the definitive biographies of those poets. I think I received a five-thousand-dollar stipend to do each of these. What could be better than to spend six weeks in Amherst with twelve other high school teachers, mostly English teachers, engaged in passionate discussion of poets and ideas under the direction of a major American scholar? I tell you about this not to stress my love of poetry but rather to make you aware of the NEH and remind you that such experiences offer important opportunities to retreat, renew, and reflect during the summer months. The six weeks studying the Psalms were especially meaningful to me, as my father was dying of cancer during those months: every psalm seemed a meditation on his trials, a lament in my father's voice, yet a celebration of the transcendence of such pain. During that summer, while reading the Psalms, we studied Walter Brueggemann's notion of the psalm cycle, something I have kept with me these many years and that applies profoundly to your own trials this year.

Briefly, Brueggemann saw life as divided into three phases that correspond to three different types of psalm: orientation, disorientation, and new orientation. Orientation refers to things as we know them: a world we understand, that is familiar; it is the world in which we feel competent, confident. In short, we know how that world works and understand our place within it. Then something comes along—a change, a new job, a new challenge (e.g., your assignment this year, my first ever AP class this year)—and causes in us a deep sense of disorientation. We lose our bearings, our confidence, our place. We become like a plains farmer wandering lost in the chaos of a snowstorm. Such moments are characterized by doubts about whether we should ever have become teachers, fear that we will not succeed, despair that we will never find our way back home to that feeling of orientation we so enjoyed. It is precisely at this darkest moment of doubt, however, that something often happens that creates a *new orientation*, a new vision of who we are or should be, what we can or must do. Disorientation feels like Psalm 22: "My God, My God, why hast thou forsaken me? Why art thou so far from helping me, and from the words of my roaring? Oh my God, I cry in the daytime, but thou hearest me not; and in the night season, and am not silent." But new orientation sounds more like the speaker in Shakespeare's twenty-ninth sonnet:

> When, in disgrace with fortune and men's eyes,
> I all alone beweep my outcast state
> And trouble deaf heaven with my bootless cries
> And look upon myself and curse my fate,
> Wishing me like to one more rich in hope,
> Featured like him, like him with friends possess'd,
> Desiring this man's art and that man's scope,
> With what I most enjoy contented least;
> Yet in these thoughts myself almost despising,
> Haply I think on thee, and then my state,
> Like to the lark at break of day arising

From sullen earth, sings hymns at heaven's gate;
For thy sweet love remember'd such wealth brings
That then I scorn to change my state with kings.

I realize as I wrap up this letter that several strands in my own life come together at this point. While in Wisconsin that summer, studying the Psalms, I was finishing up my first book, which was about my first five years of teaching (and entirely unpublishable). Still, I wrote that book as a collection of letters to the young teacher I was, letters about some of the subjects we've discussed in these letters. (It is so much easier to write to a real person!) Returning to that manuscript tonight, I found this one passage that seemed relevant to so much of what I have discussed tonight in this letter. Going away to Wisconsin allowed me to reflect on my work; the Psalms taught me about Breuggemann's psalm cycle but also about poetry; and poetry, and the study of it that summer, helped me enter deeper into the community of teachers who love their work, teachers from all over the country, from big cities and small towns, old nuns in black habits and young men ripe for love, all gathered around a table in a university united in a love of the same thing: poetry.

Here then, is a page from that book about those first five years written by me to myself:

Watching an interview of Maya Angelou this evening, I marveled at a line she spoke, for it is so true: "We must have the strength to re-create ourselves every day." I should like to hang that over my door so that each morning as I rise I can enter into the day with that thought in mind. You catch me on a day of weakness, when fatigue, frustration from recent events, and other nameless factors had me earlier at wit's end.

Today I realized, with reluctance and frustration, that there are days when the kids see me as less than human. Perhaps it is part of their psychology that they see us standing up there as some sort of pillar who will remain steady and strong as their shifting world swirls around them daily. I don't know. As if my biology had overridden my senses, I seemed unable to control my mood and was quite obviously bent out of shape, unwilling to give in. I did not like being that way. I did not enjoy myself. How can I force them to recognize that like them, I am human, that I have weaknesses, something it is important to realize that everyone has? Certainly you must feel the same thing, this being your first year. Yet I feel no less the amateur for having experience. As Rilke said, we are forever beginners; and every day I walk into that class I feel the truth of that all too keenly. This is the feeling one must surrender to if they are to go in there and re-create themselves, to walk the wire between failure and success. Isn't the challenge of it all what pumps the otherwise reluctant blood?

I bring this all up in response to some recent question about whether as a teacher I ever get depressed or not, if I ever share your frustrations. We all do. That is why it is so important that we maintain this correspondence, for it provides us both with a private place to go and try to understand the world we live in and struggle to create in our classrooms day after day.

How strange that an imaginary correspondence between the young teacher I was and the emerging teacher I had become should so anticipate our correspondence a decade later. Enjoy the book, and let me know which poem you like best when you have read some of it.

Your colleague,

Jim

Interlude 3

An Email Exchange: Absences, Subs, and an Invitation to Breakfast

⌒

Hi Joy,

Did you make it to work today? Just checking to see that all is well. Hope to see you tomorrow.

Jim

~~~~~~

Hey Jim,

No I didn't make it to work today. I called in sick because my back is giving me lots of grief. I took my little sisters out trick-or-treating last night and walked/stood/quickly walked too much. Thus, I have been in more than usual amounts of pain (and I am allergic to all sorts of meds and so can't find much relief except through old-fashioned methods of rest). Better or not I will be there tomorrow . . . one day is hard enough to miss.

Thanks for checking in.

Joy

~~~~~~

Jim,

This week doesn't seem to hold much relief for my back. I was hit by a car (the driver was trying to catch up with the driver of a stolen Porsche), and am hurting really badly (the back, oh the lower back) and may not be at work tomorrow. Luckily my car is not damaged too badly and I am not seriously injured. Thus, I may send you an e-mail that will have sub instructions.

Thanks for all your help!

Joy

~~~~~~

Joy,

You had a great sub (Marlene McBride, one of the best) and I stayed on to clarify the situation. Kids care about you as I could tell.

Get some rest; watch a good silly movie.

Jim

~ ~

Jim,

Thank you for silencing the worries I had about being gone on Friday. I am always nervous the sub will disregard all instruction and do something else (aka Mr. Powers, a sub for Santa Cruz High who would tell the kids he didn't like the lesson and would make them do something artistic and very off topic). Some of my students really hate me right now, but I am glad that some of them were concerned.

I am trying to take it easy; yet, the pain persists. See you on Monday.

Joy

~ ~

Joy,

I don't know if this is something you feel the need for, but we never have time to sit down and talk through teaching. The letters are fine—I love writing them—but sometime it might be helpful for you to sit down and work through something in a conversation. I have plans most of the day Thursday, but if you wanted to meet in Burlingame for an early breakfast that could last for a couple hours (e.g., 8–10) I'd be happy to come on down. I wouldn't offer if I didn't want to do it (or wasn't willing), so you should (1) feel free to say no for whatever reason or (2) say yes if you want to meet. If not now, we could try some other time when the stars (and schedules) align themselves.

Take care and have faith—in yourself and the kids.

Jim

~ ~

This is just to say
That the eggs
Were so
Delicious
And
The conversation
Anything but
Scrambled.

See you tomorrow.

Jim

~ ~

Jim,

As I work on school-related items throughout the day I am often reminded of how much I appreciate your participation in my growth/journey as a teacher. I often thank God that I am not left on my own, allowing my fears of inadequacy to rule. Your encouragement, guidance, resources, and so much more are vital to my progress and I am indebted to you for all your assistance.

I was reading Ecclesiastes a few days ago. If you are familiar with this book of the Bible it is basically discussing the value of all that we do or rather the lack of value in what we do ("vanity of vanities, all is vanity"). Ultimately the book discusses a few things that are valuable. One passage states: "Here is what I have seen: It is good and fitting for one to eat and drink, and to enjoy the good of all his labor in which he toils under the sun all the days of his life which God gives him; for it is his heritage" (Eccl. 5:18). I immediately thought of you when I read this passage. All your hard work and dedication to your students in and out of the classroom *and* your commitment to helping poor teachers like myself require a firm dedication to the work that you signed up for so many years ago. It is my hope that you will fully enjoy the good of all your labor as it truly is a heritage you are building, a heritage of changed lives (better students and better teachers).

Thanks so much for all you do.

Joy

~

Dear Joy:

What a pleasure it was to meet for breakfast the other day and talk about teaching over our spinach omelets on a cold, rainy day. You gave me so much to think about that I decided to write it up so I can better understand what we discussed.

Driving home, I listened to a fascinating interview with a famous improvisational acting coach who said he asks himself (and teaches his students to ask) the same question we did this morning: What works and why? He said that after a performance, or even a rehearsal of a routine, he stops and asks himself when he felt it was going well, what he was enjoying most, what gave him the most energy during the performance; then he studies it, tries to figure out what made it so effective so he can not just repeat it but apply and adapt it in future performances.

You seem to have done some useful analysis of your class by way of coming to understand how *they* work. As we discussed, you teach three of your classes in the three most difficult periods of the day: fourth (before lunch), fifth (after lunch), and sixth (at the end of the day). I thought it was also interesting that you found they did not work well *together* on Mondays and Fridays, though I think some of the things we discussed later on could improve that. You commented on some insightful differences between boys and girls, noting their different needs and attitudes; you also noted some interesting differences between kids at Burlingame, who challenge you and speak out, and those at Mills, who tend to be more passive and obedient, perhaps a reflection (from what I have heard over the years) of the predominantly Asian culture at that school.

I heard you mention several traits common to the assignments and lessons that worked:

- You had a clear vision of what you were trying to accomplish and how a particular activity or sequence of activities would lead to that outcome. In other words, you knew where you were going, knew it was the right place to go, and chose the best means of getting there.

- You allowed them some measure of choice whenever possible, thus permitting them to invest in the experience by connecting to their own lives and previous learning.

- You prepared them in each step for the next, so they consistently felt supported and ready to succeed; this allowed them to begin one step confident that it would prepare them for the next and then take that next step, assured that what they just did laid the foundation for their continued success.

- You designed activities to maintain structure in the experience while at the same time generating energy through the interaction (within groups or the class at large).

- You got them to ask questions in order to answer yours or those posed by authors in the books and articles you had them read. Thus the class is one in which kids must be "generative thinkers," something Judith Langer found was common in all effective literacy instruction.

- You broke the experience into manageable units that allowed you greater flexibility (e.g., to let them keep at it if they were engaged by a certain question or idea) and kept them engaged because they were working in a purposeful way to accomplish a clearly defined end that interested them (e.g., answering the question "What is a phony?" when reading *Catcher in the Rye*).

- You used a variety of types of texts—quotes, poems, articles, letters, books—that were related to an overarching theme or concept; these shorter texts allowed kids to read and respond to the text within the class using a range of techniques that led to a successful sequence.

- You had them respond to (or process) the ideas and information in different ways: reading, writing, talking, and representing (through performance and drawing). This not only allowed kids to find one or more entry points to get into the subject but also gave kids with different strengths (or what Stenberg calls "learning styles" and Gardner refers to as "intelligences") the opportunity to succeed.

- You had them read these shorter pieces in a more active way, asking them to annotate the text in certain ways, to answer certain questions, to prepare for certain activities; to read with a pencil in the hand is to be an active reader and thus better understand what you are reading.

- You modeled how to do what you wanted them to do so they knew, on these successful occasions, what a successful performance looked like; thus they were prepared to succeed because they knew what they were trying to do and how to do it.
- You used discussion effectively to promote engagement, to develop and maintain a community within the class, to involve all students (since it is hard to have a full-class discussion with thirty-five students, as you have).
- You watched for and noticed when they were engaged and merited more time because they were involved in a good discussion about some detail from the text; you saw the window of opportunity, and instead of saying to yourself, "No, we have to stop and do *x* now," you watered what wanted to grow, you fed the fire that they started.

Some of the things you said you still need to learn, which we can discuss more in the future, include

- How long it takes to do certain activities. I remember only too well bringing in the lesson plan I had slaved over all weekend, one I thought would take three days and result in brilliant work, only to find that it was done and going nowhere else after only *fifteen minutes*, leaving me to wonder not only what happened but what we would do with the remaining half hour. Of course the other side is when the five-minute activity takes off and suddenly fills the whole period.
- How to respond when the lesson plan that works in one period bombs in another or goes in a different direction than you anticipated.
- How to manage thirty-five rambunctious sophomores all huddled around each other in the close confines of (in our case) a portable classroom with pale light, too-hot/too-cold air, and "senior funk!" as your kids immediately shout every day as they enter, wrinkling their noses and waving their hands.

Our discussion came in the midst of some other work I have been doing on this subject of effective teaching. I include here the twenty-five teaching reminders I came up with for this other project, some of which are touched upon in my previous comments. I gave you a down payment on these the other day at breakfast but have since added more and revised those academic habits of mind I already gave you. Here they are:

1. Require students to read and write a variety of types of texts for different purposes.

2. Give students the skills, language, and knowledge they need to succeed on an assignment and participate in a discussion or activity.

3. Provide multiple entry points (i.e., via different methods, means, and media) to help students gain access to and develop a fluent understanding of the ideas, texts, and skills you teach.

4. Use the gradual release model of instruction in which the teacher models, guides, and then monitors students as they move toward independent application of concepts and skills.

5. Provide effective models that illustrate what a successful performance looks like and *explain how you achieved that result.*

6. Organize your lessons for maximum clarity (focus), understanding (comprehension), fluency (application), and recall (memory for future use).

7. Help students master a few key strategies to increase fluency and confidence across a variety of situations.

8. Maintain high expectations for *all* students *while teaching them a variety of strategies to meet those expectations.*

9. Teach students to use a variety of strategies to do their work, but also explain how, when, and why to use each strategy.

10. Connect content to previous units of study in this and other classes, to their personal lives, and to the world at large.

11. Integrate test preparation into instruction.

12. Teach students the Academic Essentials (see Figure 14.1).

13. Require students to generate ideas, hypotheses, examples—to be generative thinkers in general.

14. Teach and require students to collaborate in order to solve complex problems related to reading, writing, and thinking.

15. Demystify the elements of a successful performance in any domain, on any assignment.

16. Have students reflect on their performance and the processes they use to complete a task, especially those they are learning; have them begin by asking: What worked, what did *not*—and why?

17. Use talk to create a community, engage students, and construct meaning.

18. Organize curriculum around extended conversations about ideas that are important to the society and the students.

19. Create an intellectually active, rigorous culture in your classroom where minds synthesize, analyze, evaluate, apply, connect, and reflect.

20. Provide regular opportunities for students to perform their knowledge through discussions, presentations, publications, and more. These should be occasions to which they must rise, experiences that lead to feelings of satisfaction, pride, and achievement.

21. Begin where students *are* and then help them move along that continuum toward increasingly complex and independent performances.

22. Increase the level of difficulty consistently as students show signs of mastering the current level.

23. Provide timely and effective feedback that addresses demonstrated needs.

24. Provide students with opportunities to choose (e.g., what they read, what they write or write about) whenever possible so as to increase engagement.

25. Develop students' academic habits of mind; this means that students:
    - Take intellectual risks by experimenting with new ideas
    - Challenge their own and others' assumptions by posing provocative questions
    - Consider a subject—idea, text, author, character, result—from different perspectives, including (or especially) those different from their own
    - Participate in and contribute to academic discussions
    - Generate hypotheses, claims, and connections
    - Seek clarification or guidance when they do not understand what something means or what they are trying to say (e.g., in a paper)
    - Come to class on time with the necessary materials and their work completed
    - Give priority to facts over feelings; respect information over intuitions when writing about or discussing academic subjects

- Maintain high expectations regarding the quality of their work and effort in class and on all assignments
- Accept responsibility for their own learning

I learned much from our breakfast. Teachers so rarely get time to talk, to think about their work. I read some years ago about how copy machine technicians in a region routinely met at the same restaurant for lunch. They took long lunches during which they would no doubt discuss the latest sports scores and personal escapades, but they spent most of their time talking about problems they encountered in the field that morning. Fred would ask the group if anyone had ever encountered a broken such and such on a 1995 model 2345. Apparently the company found out about these long lunches and ended them, implementing new accountability measures to ensure maximum time on the job. Except what happened was that almost immediately the number of complaints and problems rose, for reasons quite obvious to the repair specialists: they had lost their daily troubleshooting session, their chance to exchange professional intelligence. Think about how this applies to our own work: We get about thirty minutes for lunch, much of which gets used for talking to kids, getting our lunch out, finding our way to the department office. And you have to use *yours* to zip over to Mills (preferably without having some lunatic run into you while chasing after the guy who just stole his Porsche) so you can get ready to teach fifth and sixth periods.

This is why our ongoing conversation through these letters is so special, for even I feel this same isolation, all the more so this year, for we are too locked away in these portables: there are no halls to stroll out into, no Diane McClain to wander next door and say Hi to when I saw her door open and the lights on after school.

Now it is time for me to get down to work, to get those papers scored and grades finished so I can turn them in to the office Tuesday. This last third of the semester has its own blessings and burdens, by the way: it zips by, interrupted and aided by the different holidays and events at school; it also gets a bit difficult with certain kids as they realize that their mistakes of the first two grading periods have made it nearly impossible for them to earn the grade they want ("But Mr. Burke, if I don't get at least a C in your class I won't be able to get my driver's license!") or to even pass the class, which means mandatory summer school and inevitable unhappiness.

The division of the year into two semesters is useful for students *and* teachers. Everyone needs a chance to start over, to begin anew with everything possible. You have done so many things right and well this semester; in six weeks, you can, to borrow a golfing metaphor, stop off at the club-house and take a breather, look back over the score card for the front nine before heading out the play the back nine holes, your pockets filled with all you learned from the mistakes and successes from the first half of the game. As the notes earlier in this letter show, you know what you are doing and will learn how to do it better and more consistently the longer you do it.

Thanks again for the breakfast and conversation, Joy.

Your colleague,

Jim

It appears that there are many different teacher personalities in the classroom. This may be difficult to answer, but what do you think are the different teacher personalities that are successful? Any thoughts?

Dear Joy:

This is a wonderful question and I'm glad you asked it. It shows real insight into an aspect of teaching that no one teaches because you probably *can't* teach it; you can only provide room and reason to reflect on the kind of teacher one is and wants to be. Your question also taps into some of the tension we feel when we teach material or use methods that conflict with our own beliefs. Psychologists call this divided state "cognitive dissonance." In short, it means that our actions (what we are *doing*) are not consistent with what we believe (what we *value* or *know* to be true). Finally, there is simply the reason each of us entered the profession, the image we had in our mind of our work, what it would be, the way we would experience it—compared with the reality of our job as we know it. This gets pretty abstract pretty fast, so let me take your question as an invitation to think through my own dilemma this year, for it has been on my mind for months.

I come to school every day very prepared to be a successful, effective, and, for want of a better word, "great" teacher like those who inspired me to enter the profession. They say Tiger Woods grew up imagining himself walking down the fairway with Arnold Palmer and Jack Nicklaus, *seeing* himself as their peer and then working to make himself worthy of their company. Well, I'm no Tiger Woods, but I want to honor what Pat Hanlon, Rosemary Patton, Bill Robinson, Carol Jago, and Bill Clawson taught me by being worthy of sitting at the dinner table with them; so in my own way, I try to be the kind of teacher *I* want to be while ensuring that they would approve. And after fifteen years, I have taught every class my school has offered, reaching this year what is supposed to be the pinnacle, the peak, the brass ring we all are supposed to reach for on the merry-go-round: the Advanced Placement literature course for seniors.

I worked *so* hard all summer to prepare—even *before* summer, having begun to prepare as soon as I heard in May that I would teach the course. And I've done work in the class these four months that I am proud of. And I love the kids. And I have learned more than both my hands can hold. And yet it is my work with the struggling students, those unruly works-in-progress in my ACCESS program, that I go home thinking about most at day's end; and it is your overeager crew of mixed-up sophomores who spill into the classroom as I pack up whom I look at and think, "These are my people, they are the ones I want to teach, who remind me why I became a teacher, who give me the greatest sense of purpose and deepest pleasure." When I think about my AP class, I find myself focusing on all that *I* learn, and how satisfying *I* find it to learn so much, for I love learning as I love nothing else; yet I go home every day wondering if this is the teacher I really am and am supposed to be, asking myself whom I entered the teaching profession to serve, to *teach*. I know who I am when I plan for and walk in the room to teach ACCESS students or kids like those in your sophomore class. In my AP class, and to a lesser extent during the last few years that I taught the freshman honors English class, I know what I am expected to be, for it is spelled out by the College Board, by the community, and by the parents. So just as you spend this year figuring out who you are as a teacher, what kind of teacher you want to be, I travel alongside you, asking the same questions.

Perhaps it is not such an either-or proposition as I suggest. Jennifer, a new teacher at school this year, told me she spent the last ten years working with kids very much like those in my ACCESS program but felt, after those many years, that she needed to grow, to be a different type of teacher than that class could allow her to be. Thus she came here, to teach at a more suburban, more successful school, one whose culture is defined more by its actual achievements than the pressure to achieve that dogs schools like the one Jennifer left. This brings up another aspect of the question you ask: the teacher's own need to succeed and to work within the conditions that will permit or least not prevent such success. For no matter what kind of teacher one wants to be, they will not last if they do not experience success or the promise of it sometime in the near future.

Much of what I am discussing here has to do with our identity as teachers, that is, our professional identity as defined by the setting (urban, suburban, rural, reservation), level (AP, honors/advanced, regular/college prep, remedial/lower level), type ("gifted," "college bound," "alternative"), grade (elementary, middle, high school, college), subject (English, physics, P.E.), kids (good, cool, hard, fun, caring, easy), and, increasingly, the state ("highly qualified teacher," Board Certified Teacher).

I remember first thinking about these questions of teacher persona when I was still in the teaching credential program. A woman I often sat next to had been assigned to a nice suburban school with a good reputation. One night she said she wasn't sure she would complete the program because she did not go into teaching to teach those kids. Sure, of course, she cared for them and enjoyed them, but she grew up in the city, in an urban environment, and wanted to be an urban teacher. Her comments made me think of my own teaching assignment very differently, for I was dividing my day between teaching every morning at Lowell High School, one of the most prestigious, academically rigorous public schools in the nation and then running around the corner to teach at Bay High, a small alternative public school where every kid had a parole officer and lived in a court-appointed group home. As a result of this experience, I developed early on a sense of commitment to kids at both ends of the continuum, finding in both a set of unique, meaningful challenges that allowed me to learn what interested me most while helping them at the same time.

I feel as though I am circling around my prey, the answer to the question you ask, but not closing in for the kill to make the point. I think this is because I find myself realizing that we negotiate with ourselves throughout our career as a teacher, trying on different personae and, upon reflection, asking ourselves if that was a good fit. I heard once (it doesn't really matter if it's actually true) about an elite teacher of high school government (aka civics) whose walls were covered with campaign pins, posters, and other memorabilia he had collected. He was a complete junkie for all things political. He taught the AP government class until a new principal joined the faculty. This principal came in and told the government teacher that he had heard he was a great teacher; he also told him that he didn't believe courses belonged to teachers, that all kids deserved to have access to the best teachers, so he was reassigning him to teach some lower-level, perhaps even remedial, course. The teacher immediately quit, saying simply that he had entered teaching to work with the best and the brightest, and he left to work at an elite private school. While it's easy to engage with the teacher's stance, even dismiss him as arrogant or a prima donna, the point is that he knew who he was and what he wanted from his experience in the classroom. When you are up at midnight (as we can be on occasion) or working all day on a nice Sunday (such as I see outside my window today), responding to student papers or preparing to teach a new novel, you must believe in what you are doing, must see that work as an expression of who you are or are trying to be.

To return to your initial question about identity, I see several different types of teachers, or perhaps one might better understand them as roles. You raise the question of the "authoritative" teacher, but there is also the *authoritarian* teacher, who rules, dictates, controls by one means or another. One (the authoritative teacher) knows their stuff while the other knows the rules. Of course there are other distinctions: easy, hard, and in between. But none of these descriptions captures the inherent complexity of our work as teachers, so I find it more helpful to consider the roles we must play if we are to be considered effective, excellent teachers. I see the following roles, all of which excellent teachers find a way to balance within themselves, if not at all times, at least over the course of the day, week, or month:

- Master
- Coach
- Parent/counselor
- Entertainer
- Specialist
- Leader
- Student
- Enforcer
- Traditionalist
- Innovator

Some of these roles establish and maintain our credibility in the eyes of the students and the larger community. A sense of mastery—knowing and being able to do well what we teach kids to do—is essential, for it inspires in students the confidence needed to follow us, to accept our teaching. Yet within that sense of mastery must also remain the sense that you are a student of the game, one who continues to study and learn more about your subject out of a combination of personal curiosity and professional commitment. This continued study might focus on one area, such as the teacher's specialty; such strength helps to create in students a sense of wonder and respect for the breadth of the teacher's knowledge, further enhancing that teacher's credibility. While some roles matter—most notably parent/counselor and entertainer—they are not necessary and can, in some cases, undermine one's effectiveness in the classroom. In most surveys I have read or heard about, kids always respect the teacher who comes to be a teacher, not to be their friend. Though I would make one comment about this: kids need to believe that you are actually committed to them, that you like and care about them as people.

As for style, I think it's important to create a balance between being innovative and traditional; they are not mutually exclusive but should complement each other in meaningful ways. For example, kids know the world is changing and expect you to prepare them for the world they will live in, not the one you grew up in. Innovation can take many forms, but it should be effective and meaningful. Technology is an obvious means of being innovative, but it can be counterproductive when used in meaningless or ineffective ways that waste time. The other day, for example, I saw clusters of kids I taught years before moving around campus with video cameras. They were spending a few days filming images for short videos related to a novel they were reading. While there is surely good stuff that could be done with such an important book, the kids only rolled their eyes and smirked when I asked them what they were doing and why; they had no clear purpose and saw the whole thing as a waste; they were accomplishing nothing that would yield pride or knowledge. So the teacher's efforts to be innovative were undermined by the lack of context and purpose that came at the expense of more traditional needs such as how to write in ways the kids had not yet mastered or read at still deeper levels.

Throughout all these roles, however, one is of particular importance to me: the leader. What else are we if not leaders of a small city called our classroom, whose citizens are our students and whose constitution consists of the dreams they want us to help them realize? A business book, *Lincoln on Leadership*, by Donald Phillips, is one of my favorite books because it examines the qualities that made Lincoln a successful leader in tough times, one who brought people together in a common purpose for a greater good.[1] Here are, according to Phillips, Lincoln's core "strategies," organized by category:

PEOPLE

- Get out of the office and circulate among the troops
- Build strong alliances
- Persuade rather than coerce

CHARACTER

- Honesty and integrity are the best policies
- Never act out of vengeance or spite
- Have the courage to handle unjust criticism
- Be a master of paradox

ENDEAVOR

- Exercise a strong hand—be decisive
- Lead by being led
- Set goals and be results-oriented
- Keep searching until you find your "Grant"
- Encourage innovation

COMMUNICATION

- Master the art of public speaking
- Influence people through conversation and storytelling
- Preach a vision and continually reaffirm it

Sticking with history and its lessons for a moment more, I share, to confirm much of what I have said, this passage from a short article in *Education Week* a few years back:

> At every level of education, there is a recurrent question: What constitutes good teaching? Some years ago, I embarked on an interesting bit of research in pursuit of an answer to that query. As a historian, I decided to explore the autobiographies of prominent Americans from the 19th and 20th centuries (some 125 of them). As these people—men and women of different social, economic, geographic, religious, and racial backgrounds—recounted their educational experiences, what did they have to say about teachers whom they valued?
>
> The single most notable discovery was the extraordinarily consistent pattern in the description of the good teacher. I guess I would have to say good and *memorable* teacher. There were three characteristics that were described time and again—to an astonishing degree: competence in the subject matter, caring deeply about students and their success, and character, distinctive character. These attributes were evident regardless of the level of education or the subject matter being taught.[2]

So we come to the subject that Diane McClain and I have discussed for years, ever since she began teaching the public-speaking class and I began giving more public speeches: ethos. It's one of those words I heard for years and couldn't quite puzzle out, like its siblings *pathos* and *bathos*. I figured that people who used these words were showing off their Greek. But *ethos* is different. Figure 10.1 shows a diagram from the speech book Diane uses.

It sums up in one simple diagram the key elements I have discussed here while wandering around in and trying to give an answer to your question. I

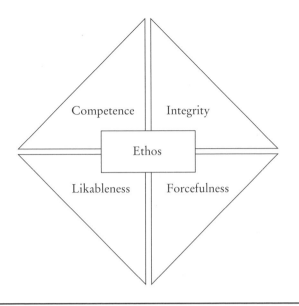

FIGURE 10.1[3]

could tell you there are six types of teacher, or eight, or three, but in the end there is only the teacher you will spend your life trying to become, one that is made up of the student you were, the teachers who inspired you to enter teaching, and those you'll meet along the way who will leave a lasting impression on you. And so I end with only this by way of a final effort to answer your question: every day that you work the way you do gets you closer to this place you seek, and every day that you work this way you give your students the best lesson, the one they will remember—do what you need to do and do it well no matter how long it takes.

In the meantime, you bring dignity to this profession of ours and make me proud to call myself a teacher.

It was Thanksgiving this week, so give thanks for all you have done, all you have learned and will learn in the months ahead. The weeks to come will blizzard past, and before you know it the first semester will be done. Then you can take time to look back on all that you did to learn what will help you do even better with all that is to come.

Your colleague,

Jim

Do you have any essay-writing books that you would suggest a teacher have? I'm looking for something:
  - A bit anti-five-paragraph essay
  - With helpful, clear instructions
  - Useful for me to assist students with their writing skills while steering them away from the five-paragraph essay format I recall learning in elementary school

～

Dear Joy:

Yet another important question, one everyone thinks about but few people discuss openly: the use of structures to help kids learn to write. But your question, as usual, has other aspects, raises other issues: the importance of professional reading, the question of which books are worth buying and actually reading, the role of writing instruction in the larger curriculum.

I will try to answer these different questions by focusing on the different types of books I read, how I read them, and when I actually find time do so. Today, as it happens, is a perfect day to think about these issues, for I have been reading student papers all day. With this in mind, let me start by telling you when I do some of my most satisfying and useful professional reading: in short gulps before I start responding to papers or, on other occasions, before I sit down to plan my lessons. I have several books going at one time, each with a different focus, so I ask myself what I should focus on, what I need to do a better job of when I read the papers or create the lesson plan. Today, for example, I decided I would see what Vicki Spandel says about responding to student papers in the new edition of her incredible book *Creating Writers*.

This kind of reading is some of the most useful there is for me. It's purposeful: I am coming to the book with a specific question I want answered or a subject about which I want to learn more. I read until I find something I can use; then I shelve the book and get to work. I think of this as personal professional development (PPD), something most schools (ours included) do a terrible job of providing. So what do I get for my fifteen-minute investment? Aside from an excellent comparison of comments that do and don't help, and the traits of effective remarks, I learn that there are three primary types of response: questions, comments, and concerns. To these, Spandel adds two more that can grow out of the first three: conversations and conferences (about the piece of writing or some aspect of it).

I keep a few of my favorites handy, right on my desk for quick reference or casual study between papers or while some long document is printing out. The point I want to make is that it doesn't matter so much *what* you read as *that* you read. Don Graves or Don Murray, Fran Claggett or Lucy Calkins, Ralph Fletcher or Carol Jago, Nancie Atwell or Peter Elbow—these are all great teachers, experienced guides for us to follow, but what matters most is to join the conversation they, too, are a part of, to which they contribute through their writings. We too easily excuses ourselves from our own learning, begging off with the excuse of no time, no energy, too many papers, and the high cost of books.

So you buy one book, a book like Donald Murray's *Write to Learn*, a book you cannot help but love for its familiar voice and practical wisdom. And you read it for ten minutes a day, or whenever you can, until you finish. This is how I read most professional books: early in the morning, over cereal and coffee, meditating on some aspect of reading or writing, teaching or thinking. No rush to finish it; in fact, loving the patience with which I have learned to read these books. Some books are better for snippets, because they are designed to be read that way. Ralph Fletcher and Joanne Portaluppi's *Craft Lessons* is such a book, giving you a nice neat lesson on one page; so within three minutes you can learn something worth more than the price of the book.

There are different kinds of books to read, however. You can, and should, read books about the teaching of writing. Such books include Murray's *Write to Learn*, Spandel's *Creating Writers*, Jago's *Cohesive Writing*, Dombek and Herndon's *Critical Passages*, and Atwell's *Lessons That Change Writers* or *In the Middle*. Oh, and my own book *Writing Reminders*, of course! These focus on how to *teach* writing, something few teachers are actually taught. Other books, no less important, focus on writing: what it is, how it works, what writers do. Strunk and White's *Elements of Style* gets top honors from many in this category; some even suggest reading it every year. Zissner's *On Writing Well* is another, a classic of coherent writing *about* writing. Joe Williams' *Style: Ten Lessons in Clarity and Grace* is a personal favorite of mine. That book is so polished in its insights and advice that you cannot dip your toe into it without learning something. There are other, more commercial, popular books about writing that are no less helpful and interesting. Stephen King's *On Writing* comes to mind; he braids discussion of craft and life together in a highly entertaining and thoughtful meditation on writing. Annie Lamott does something similar, though with more humor, in her book *Bird by Bird*. And the *New York Times* has published a series of columns that have been released as books called *Writers on Writing*, in which, surprise, respected writers reflect on different aspects of their craft. Great stuff. What is the moral of the story? You must know about writing—how it works, how it's created—to really teach it well.

There are other, more technical books you will want to read over time, but these are best read when you have a few years tucked into your back pocket and are ready for the next level of learning. Such books are more specific, dealing with syntax or style, grammar or punctuation. Some are very dense but also rich in material. Edward P. J. Corbett and Robert Connors' *Classical Rhetoric for the Modern Student*, for example, or its slimmer version, which contains only Chapter 4, called *Style and Statement*. *The Craft of Research*, by Wayne Booth, Gregory Columb, and Joseph Williams, is brilliant; I learned so much about argument and questioning from it. You can look at more specialized books about writing poetry, essays, fiction, or literary response. And it's important to have one authoritative source for all technical information; in this case, I have to go with *The St. Martin's Handbook*, by Andrea Lunsford, in the latest edition available.

As I said, with these books, it is not so much about reading them all as about getting into the conversation about our craft, running your own little workshop with one of these books as companion and mentor through whatever terrain you decide is most important. If you want one to buy yourself for Christmas, go with either Vicki Spandel's *Creating Writers* or Carol Booth Olson's *The Reading/Writing Connection*. These are both focused on how to *teach* writing and approach writing as a teachable skill.

One last thing before I check out for the night: You have to write yourself. It keeps you honest about the struggle to create language. *You* try "jotting down some insightful observations about the way in which two characters change," and suddenly you feel a bit woozy, wondering how to start, what to say, how to say it—and you're the teacher! If nothing else, you can always write with your kids in class, even if for only part of the time. But you can also write for a larger audience, something I never thought to do until I went to a conference and, while talking over lunch with another teacher, was told I should write about what I had been discussing. Of course it takes time, but it's worth it. Here, by way of a conclusion, is one of the first essays I ever wrote about teaching. I thought you might enjoy it because I saw that you had just passed out *Catcher in the Rye* to the kids (or were you collecting it from them?).

AT THE COLISEUM

Jim Burke

I should have realized that something was askew when, during a class discussion of *The Catcher in the Rye*, I found myself identifying more with Mr. Antolini, Holden Caulfield's schoolteacher, than with Holden himself. But that morning, I didn't yet comprehend that the past two years of teaching high school English had caused a subtle shift within me, leaving me on new, unfamiliar ground. So when one of my students, an amiable young woman who had also been in my class last year, asked if my wife and I would be interested in going to a concert with her and a few friends, I accepted. I was touched by the offer and moved by its meaning: To her, I was a human being, someone who transcended the one-dimensional realm of our classroom.

We discussed plans for the 12-hour music festival. My wife and I would make main course dishes, and my student and her friends would provide snacks, munchies, and blankets. We would meet them around noon. My wife and I are both 29 years old and in our second year of teaching. We find ourselves growing into a new phase of our lives: adulthood. It's a phase that gives us a frightening influence over people half our age, people who are growing up on the music of bands we first heard in college. On the drive down, we decided that we would shelve the Mr. and Mrs. routine for the day and just be Jim and Susan, two concert-goers enjoying music with our friends.

A little after noon, we found ourselves at a concert featuring every style of pop music: rap (Queen Latifah and Ice-T), heavy metal (the Charlatans UK and Steve Jones, formerly of the Sex Pistols), acoustic (Michelle Shocked and Indigo Girls), and punk (the Cramps and Iggy Pop). I began to realize that things on the music scene had changed since I last attended a concert when Lux Interior, lead singer of the Cramps, pulled off his pants and stood atop the stage in a leather jockstrap and lavender pumps, swigging from a bottle of wine and sucking on his microphone. I stood behind my student and her friends and watched them dance and laugh at the act, which they were obviously enjoying. Suddenly, my 29 years felt like many, many more. My own 14th year seemed distant and idyllic, a Wizard of Oz Kansas, where the closest things got to Lux Interior was when farmers peeled off their shirts to stand bare-chested in the sun. My despair gave way to confusion when I realized, like generations of adults before me, that I found this music offensive and unnecessarily obscene. Still, I clung to the thought that I was just another concert-goer. Between acts, we all reclined and enjoyed the beautiful Saturday unfolding around us. We talked with ease, shedding our roles of student and teacher and sharing the food we had all brought. The only time I felt briefly defined by my job was when one of the girls casually asked me when progress reports would be mailed.

But when the emcee announced the next band, things got more complex. My role changed from concert-goer to observer of a culture that I could no longer rightfully claim as my own. It belonged to my students. After a pseudo-serious announcement that Ice-T could not come on because local censors had declared his show pornographic, the performer burst onto the stage with his intimidating-looking entourage. He proceeded to say that he would show the censors that being an American meant being able to do whatever you want. He went on to say that the idea of putting parental advisory stickers on record albums (uh oh, I date myself), I mean on CDs, was ridiculous. If parents were guiding their children the way they were supposed to, he said, there would be no need for stickers. Impressed by his stance, and doubly impressed that my kids were listening to such socially responsible performers, I got ready to enjoy the show.

Then, Ice-T unzipped his pants and sang the rest of the set with his bright white briefs shining like a shield. Periodically, he pulled up the sagging trousers but never zipped them. This seemed more stupid than anything else. He stopped near the end of his show to address the issue of parental and social censorship once more. "If your parents tell you you can't listen to or buy some piece of music because it's dirty," he told the audience, "you just tell your mom to 'Fuck off!'" The audience exploded with a wild roar of applause.

Completely stunned by this, I sat down with my wife. The night had settled upon us; it was time for dinner. With Ice-T's words still ringing in my ears, I retrieved my large container of pasta al pesto with artichoke hearts. In the gathering darkness, I could make out the students' incredulous looks as I doled it out. I suddenly realized that this was food I would have tried to slip to the dog when I was their age. They worked at it with gusto, however, secreting their paper plates off to the side, thinking I could not see the little oily artichoke hearts sitting there, abandoned.

Finally, the noise of the concert ended in a pulsating silence, leaving us to clean up our site and pack up the goods. I found myself worrying about these five 14- to 16-year-old girls whose parents had let them come to this concert alone. I thought back to how they had listened to Ice-T's obscenities while two lesbian women engaged in passionate, drunken sex about five feet from us. I worried that the girls' innocence was withering in my presence. And I was helpless to stop it. I felt like Holden Caulfield watching his little sister, Phoebe, reach for the golden ring on the merry-go-round, worrying that she would fall off. I wanted to be the damned catcher in the rye. I worried that these kids were growing up in a society where the poets of song have nothing instructive to say, where, as the hero of the movie *Pump Up the Volume* says, "All the great themes are gone; they've been turned into theme parks."[1]

Only two weeks until the break. Hope you had a good day grading papers with the other teachers at the district office.

Your colleague,

Jim

Question 12

Do you ever doubt yourself as a teacher and worry that you will fail?

〜

Dear Joy:

I assure you that I still get scared and that I still worry that I will not succeed as a teacher. Some things this weekend made me realize how important it is for me to continue to walk this line between the familiar and the fearful, between what I know and what I'm learning. The event that led to this realization about fear was a passing exchange between a student in my AP class and me that no one would have paid attention to had they been sitting in class that day. The event is not important (though the following letter will explain it); what mattered was that I realized something important to me about my identity as a teacher. In short, I realized that to love my work and feel proud of it and believe in what I am doing, I must be the teacher I know I am and have trained to be.

All year I have struggled within the constraints of the AP curriculum. I came to the class with such excitement about all I was learning and would be able to teach, only to find myself intimidated by the senior attitude, the faux maturity of the arrogant eighteen-year-old who thinks they have nothing left to learn. So I have felt like the characters in Saramago's novel *Blindness* who suddenly find themselves without sight, left to find their way through a world they knew so well. For me, this world has been English, the teaching of it, especially to freshman students, but this year I am in classes almost twice as large as my largest freshman class, and I'm teaching an entirely new curriculum to students I am still getting to know—so different are these seniors from the freshmen I have taught for years. I can find my way only by bumping up against the limits of my learning, fumbling forward, guided by little more than instinct and what I learn along the way. Needless to say, all this anxiety has kept me off balance, made me feel unsure of what I can do in the class, whereas with the freshmen, I knew very well, understood, and could, in fact, define the kind of relationship we would have, for that class was a country I created, whose every nuance I could name and use to good effect.

Without going on, I will let the letter to Eric explain what happened and how I responded to it. For the record, he is the top student in the school (actually, in the district), has applied to Stanford for early decision, and sits on the district's board of trustees as the student representative for kids in the district. So he is not a kid used to hearing someone tell him he is not perfect. I came so close to not sending it (I write letters that I never send, also, something I have found very therapeutic as a form of journaling) but finally decided that if I was to have any desire to teach this AP course again, I needed to be able to work with kids the way I always have: in a close, personal manner, as a coach, a mentor to their mind as well as their emerging self. Here is my initial letter:

Eric,

Sitting down to your *Hamlet* essay just now—I haven't read it yet—I couldn't help feeling a bit discouraged. I've worked long and hard on these essays, giving comments and the chance to revise when they come back. It takes a serious effort and real commitment on my part to do this part of my work; I love teaching kids to write (or do anything) better. But I need to launch into it (a paper, that is) with the belief that the student will listen, wants to learn, to improve. I realized something as I turned to your paper, and whether I'm wrong or right doesn't matter so much as the fact that it's my perception and you should listen to it. My first thought, perhaps with our exchange this morning still fresh in mind, was that you'd rather argue why you're right than learn how to get better. This was how I felt after we discussed your college essay. I made comments based on a whole lot of knowledge and experience and you left me feeling like you were going to leave it as you had it because you didn't think that it would make a difference. I have great respect for your success in school and don't mean to imply for one second that you don't work your butt off to do well. But there can be a cynicism in your tone at times that I worry will hold you back from the greater success that could be yours. You can't lead if you can't listen or learn. Today two great students of mine did poorly on that quiz: one dismissed the content as useless, irrelevant; the other sought me out, asked how does this work, what did I miss, could you explain it to me? That person sees themselves as someone able to learn anything, and sees any setback as an opportunity to learn, not a loss. That attitude will take that student to great places, in part because it invites, it makes others (e.g., teachers, colleagues, eventually bosses) want to help, to invest in that person's success. This evening your attitude makes me want to just slap an A on your paper and move on, without even reading it because I know it is good enough. But "good" is the enemy of great. You never say it's good enough on the soccer field; you say, let's go one more time. Carry that attitude with you off the field and into the world and people will follow you.

I don't take time to write letters like this to kids unless I care about them and have real faith in what they can accomplish. Reducing things, as you did this morning, to the smallest factor of why bother or what's in it for me, fosters an attitude that limits you. To lead, as you may some day, you must learn from any situation, must listen to every voice—even those with which you do not agree—and take risks, intelligent, creative risks that involve seeing what others cannot, doing what others will not. Of course you already know this: while others were home watching TV or playing video games, you were running the extra lap on the soccer field as the last light of the day leaked away; while others strolled the avenue with friends, you did twenty more minutes of drills to master that move with the left foot, not so you would win a spot on the team but so you could master the game.

I have written letters like this for years, but not in this AP class. I don't know that I have permission from you to talk to you like this. But I take these risks, and do it because it is part of what I love about my work, which is about much more than absolute phrases and comparing-contrasting. I hope you don't mind me saying what I have here. Even if you think I'm wrong, just listen—to me, to yourself, to anyone who takes you seriously enough to speak to you as the fine young man you are teaching yourself to be.

See you in the morning,
Mr. Burke

It would be embarrassing to tell you how nervous it made me to write this. As I say at the letter's end, I just didn't know if he (or others) would give me permission to write these things, to speak to him this way. But this is who I am as a teacher; doing this was one of the first expressions of who I am, the way I work in the first semester. So it was a necessary risk. But I didn't hear from Eric for four days, so I was a bit nervous when Sunday evening his response beeped its way into my email inbox. Here it is:

Mr. Burke,

First of all, thank you for caring. It means a lot to me.

Second, I apologize for my comments to you on Thursday—actually, not so much for my comments, but rather for my attitude. I did not approach the situation as well as I could have. I will try to do better in the future.

Third, and most importantly, I hope that you don't really think, as you suggested in your letter, that my poor attitude on Thursday—only one day of 180 in the year—is an accurate reflection of my overall attitude in your class or in school in general. That is simply not true. Like I stated earlier, I am not at all proud of dismissing a concept as useless and then scoring 1 of 8 on the quiz. Please understand, however, that that was the first time I have ever felt that way in your class. I was frustrated, and I wasn't shy about it. Let's be honest: you know as well as I do that 100% of students in a class are not 100% engaged in every single activity we do. Perhaps it is of some consolation to you, then, that rather than simply think to myself "Well, that was a big waste of time" and trudge off to my next class, I at least sought you out to tell you how I felt. You may not believe me, but I did not ask you about the purpose of learning these phrases to criticize your teaching or to put myself "above" such seemingly minor concepts; rather, I confronted you with the hope that you would say something that could change my mind. And you have, in retrospect, changed my attitude.

Our conversation about my college essay was very helpful, as were the comments you made on my shorter school board essay. I really mean that—you helped me a lot. You are correct, however, that I did not make the major change to my long essay that you suggested. Please don't take it personally, because I value your comments. In that particular instance, however, I did not want to completely rewrite the latter half of an essay that I had spent countless hours on, and that won 2nd place of 900 students in an essay contest. Furthermore, I had read close to 100 successful college essays before writing my own, so I had a good idea of what goes into a successful essay. Finally, I was pressed for time. I value your input greatly, but felt that I, as the author, had every right to make the ultimate decision about my essay. Yesterday I received my Stanford acceptance letter, which validates my decision to some degree. I'm not trying to put you or your advice down; I'm just explaining things from my perspective.

About my *Hamlet* essay: I hope that you read it or will read it, because I worked extremely hard on it. You will be the ultimate judge of how successful an essay it is, but I tried to make my essay not just "good," but "great." If this one wasn't "great," hopefully my next essay will be.

Again, I apologize for my conduct on Thursday. In general, however, I have been working extremely hard in your class, with an open mind and a willingness to learn. Whether you agree with this statement or not, I will continue to do so.

All the Best,
Eric Showen

I was so relieved to get his letter. It was an important confirmation of my belief that teaching is personal, that we must teach in ways that are true to our ideals (so long as they are consistent with the society's ideals). His reply gave me the permission I needed to take such risks again in the future. Here is my response to Eric's letter:

You're a good man, Eric, which is why I took time to say those things. Frankly, a guy like you gets told so often (for good reason) how good his work is, what a great student he is, that it's a good tonic to hear a voice challenge you once in awhile. We need to always feel our boundaries so we have something to push against, to overcome, to give us that sense of greater gain for our efforts. In general, my guess is that no one's expectations of you are higher than your own, which is why I respect your diligence and felt I could push a bit—because I know you are always trying to be your best. Don't listen to my letter for anything other than what it was: one of your various coaches pushing you to be as great as I know you can be.

Your letter back was just a confirmation of all that I have seen in you, Eric. Thanks for taking time to write such a thoughtful response and to take my letter as a chance to reflect. We have about six months left, and I look forward to all that I will learn from you and through this class. I must admit, after years of freshman English classes, I feel challenged in this class as I have not in some years. And as for your *Hamlet* paper, please be assured that I will give it my best—perhaps even a bit more by way of appreciation for our exchange here—as I intended to do all along

Not sure if you have read many business books, but Steven Covey, who wrote the *Seven Habits of Highly Effective People*, has a new book out that I think you might find important when you have the time (I read it in 5–10 minute bits between various work at home). It's called *The Eighth Habit: From Effectiveness to Greatness.*

I'll see you in the morning and be glad to do so. I'm grateful for the chance to work with you and learn from you this year, Eric. Back to those *Hamlet* essays!

Mr. Burke

I think the reason I am sometimes envious of your wacky sophomore class is that I know who I am and can be when I am with those kids or the kids in my ACCESS class. They are "my people," and so I know what kind of relationship I can develop, what roles I can play, how I can talk to them. I don't know if what I have said here is relevant to you and your work right now, but it seemed a useful follow-up to your earlier question about the different kinds of teachers we can be. I wrote it because this exchange of the last few days felt important to me: something was at stake, something important that I nonetheless could not easily define. Writing these letters to you helps me remember who I am trying to be, what I am trying to accomplish in that class with those kids. As Steven Covey says in his new book, our task is to "use our voice to help others find theirs." By giving me cause (and occasion) to write, you have done this for me and I am grateful for it.

Your colleague,

Jim

Question 13

How can I use what I learned from the fall semester to be a better teacher in the spring?

⤳

Dear Joy:

And so we arrive at the end of the first semester, the journey not done, but half gone, giving us both the chance to learn from all that's happened along the way. I was reminded of the importance of learning, of not only setting and having but reflecting on goals, yesterday while reading a paper I had never seen: *Investor's Business Daily*. It apparently has this incredible page every day that is devoted to leaders and success, and offers "Wisdom to Live By." The editors lead with their "Ten Secrets to Success," a list that has evolved after spending "years analyzing leaders and successful people in all walks of life." They argue that "most [leaders and successful people] have ten traits that, when combined, can turn dreams into reality." The secrets include having a positive attitude, determining specific goals and working actively and persistently to achieve them, treating others with respect and integrity, and continually striving to learn and to innovate.[1]

What impresses me most is that one can *learn* to succeed, that we can revise our story of failure into one of success, for we are the author of our days. As an English teacher I tend to think in stories: how it begins, who the players are, what themes I want to run through my story, and so on. To prepare the kids for finals, I created an organizer called the Character Arc tool (see Figure 13.1). This is a graphic representation of a fairly old idea: a character changes over the course of a story. I thought you might find this useful as a tool for teaching but also for reflecting on this first semester. I did this the other day in class with the kids; I had them use it to reflect on where they were as freshmen four years ago and where they are now as seniors. All along the arc you must note those events or experiences that *led to* the "End" words. It gave me a sense of movement—from where I was in August as an AP English teacher (inexperienced, intimidated, novice, freshman honors

CHARACTER ARC

NAME: _____ PERIOD: _____

Directions: Characters change over the course of a story; at least the important
characters do. But *how* do they change—and *why*? We should also ask
which, of all the different changes, is most important—and, of course, *why*
it is so important. Use this tool (and these questions) to analyze how the
character changes over the course of the story. You should also identify
key moments (by indicating them on the arc) that caused the changes
along the way.

PART ONE: ANALYZE

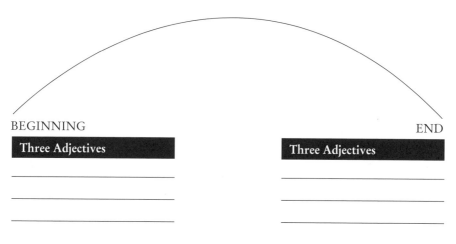

BEGINNING   END

| Three Adjectives |

| Three Adjectives |

_____

_____

_____

PART TWO: SYNTHESIZE

Directions: Use your notes and ideas from Part One to help you write a paragraph
in which you synthesize the character's changes and the causes and
significance of those changes. Be sure your paragraph has a claim,
organizes the information effectively, and provides specific examples
that illustrate and support your claim.

_____

_____

_____

_____

_____

_____

_____

FIGURE 13.1   © 2005 Jim Burke.

teacher, student) to where I am now in January (engaged, assured, committed, guide, partner [with Elaine Caret], AP teacher). I found it strangely helpful to list the events of the last semester that had led to these changes. I encourage you to do it yourself during the break between the semesters.

It is *so* easy, too easy, in fact, to look back on the semester and cringe before the mirror that shows what we would rather not see. It is painful to learn in public, as we both inevitably did these last five months. As it happens, there was an article yesterday in that same *Investor's Business Daily* edition about taming our "inner critic," something that often seems to give you trouble. Here is the opening:

> Criticism. It can be helpful in teasing out problems with products or ideas. Or, it can snag great thoughts long before they rise to the surface. How do you manage it?
>
> The most successful people learn how to retain valuable critiques as they edit criticism that keeps innovative ideas from blossoming.
>
> Learn how to dance with the critics—especially the imaginary ones that bound around in your skull—and you'll be more likely to come up with some new approaches that work even better than the ones you're using right now.[2]

As I mentioned today when we met for lunch, I had some unusually strong criticism from one student this semester. I might best sum up his three-page harangue by saying he considers me incompetent and ignorant, and said so in notably forceful language. Luckily his was a lone opinion, but still it is his voice that has taken up residence in my head these last few days. I have found such students can be useful, if frustrating at times, for they keep us honest, remind us that we are not perfect, that we are, indeed, far from it. And yet I would not take back one mistake I made, for *all* my mistakes were necessary to my learning, since only after I made them did I know they were mistakes. People tell a story of Edison: One night his warehouse caught fire. This is the place where he had *everything*, where he did all his research. His son was roused and told to get his father. Upon arriving at the scene of the blaze, seeing the building entirely consumed in flames, everything gone, Edison told his son to go get his wife. Standing before the inferno of loss, Edison put his arms around his wife and son and reportedly said something like, "This is a wonderful event to behold, for all our mistakes are in that building and tomorrow we can begin fresh, keeping only what we know works." On some other occasion, Edison said, "Results? Why I have several thousand results. I have learned of at least a thousand things that do not work." Thus, to borrow from yet another quote of Edison's, we "blunder, but blunder forward," guided by what we learn along the way so long as we stop to reflect and revise.

It is with that critical student's voice, which could never be as demanding as my own, that I have sat down these last few nights to reflect on the last semester. I did for myself what we did for you when we met some months back for breakfast: I pulled out a pad of paper and wrote down what worked and what did not; then I analyzed *why*. This was remarkably helpful as it made concrete those things I had done or could do to improve. Returning to the Character Arc diagram, I also asked myself what words I wanted to be able to put down at the end of this year, beginning with the end in mind, and then I asked myself how I would get there.

I decided that for the beginning of the second semester, anyway, I need to work more on creating a sustainable, effective but flexible instructional structure for my AP class. I want to have greater consistency in what they accomplish and the way they work. Lately we have had these excellent opening fifteen-minute sequences during which they read, write, and eventually talk about some focused aspect of the text they read the previous night for homework. They do these writings in their journals, but we make good use of them as an opportunity to work on writing as well as to improve on our discussion of literature. This is all very new to me, to be honest, but the approaching AP test forces me to think in these ways to improve efficiency and economy of instruction, not terms I typically use to describe instruction. Yet it makes sense to me as I get more intentional in my teaching. For too long teachers have been focused on activities instead of *instruction*. When I walk into my ACCESS classes, I have set goals in mind, skills I know they need to learn if they are to succeed. This helps me prepare, focus, and organize my instruction in ways that pay off. The difference such guided instruction makes is profound, as the following email shows, but this is also a class that I have taught and carefully revised for five years. I sent this note to my editor this morning after scoring the final ACCESS reading tests:

> When you teach a class like ACCESS, and especially when you just finished writing a *book* about it, it's hard to ignore scores and data. You do all these things, based on ideas and theories, principles and experience, and you give the kids formal tests like the Scholastic Reading Inventory (SRI) or the Gates, or some miscue analysis, and then you pray. You hate the scores if they don't tell the story you want; you hug them if they do. So in September I gave the Gates (required by the district) and did individual

miscues on all 25 kids in ACCESS, some of whom scored in the basement. Then yesterday I gave them the SRI, which I actually like the best, though the miscue matters, too. The SRI is hard (demands intense inferential reading) and long (70 questions with passages that are not haiku). And this morning I scored them. I stood at the scantron reader, listening to it tick like a heart monitor, a few ticks for some (good), many for others (bad), and I was getting very nervous. After all, we have spent a semester doing stuff that I claim really works. But so many red marks on some of the tests! Then I returned and converted the scores. Then I went to the cumulative data sheet with the September scores. Finally, I went through and compared today's scores with September's. If their current score was higher than *both* the September scores (Gates and miscue) I put a + next to their name. If the current score was higher than one of the two, I put an x. If the current score was lower, I put a –. Final score: + next to 24 out of 25 names, most with *significant* gains. I'm as thrilled as I am relieved!

What matters to me in this story is that I was neither teaching to a test nor running a skills workshop; we developed those skills (and will continue to do so, for this is merely confirmation that we are moving in the right direction) through authentic reading in a variety of contexts. That is what I want to be able to say about my AP class, and so I will try to create a lesson plan template that will guide me. This process of revision will help me improve the rough draft of my AP class, though I will necessarily make new mistakes, or the same mistakes for different reasons en route to a new understanding. In years to come my instruction and my students' success will begin to follow the same story line the ACCESS numbers tell. What that angry, disaffected student resented was having to live through my rough draft; he felt like a character that the author (me) keeps moving around and giving different lines to say as he figures out what he is trying to accomplish through the story he is learning to tell. In short, this student wants what no teacher can give him: a perfect performance on the first run-through. Years from now he will make mistakes as he learns his field; I can only hope he will remember his words to me and work with people who are more generous and understanding than he was with me. His expectations and resentment ignore the very nature of mastery, which must be earned through the secrets to success that I mentioned at the beginning of this letter.

Let me close by telling you—I don't know what other word to use, really—how *proud* I am of you. I know this first semester was *hard, hard, hard.* Those weeks before Winter Break were brutal; it's a hard time for everyone but hardest for a new teacher. But you have persevered, revised yourself and your craft day by day, class by class. And when you asked that troublesome boy to stay after so you could talk with him the other day, what you learned is that kids will always respond to an adult who tries to connect with them. This is the essence of our work for our students and, as we discussed, for *ourselves*. Right now, you are working hardest to find the voice that is yours as a teacher. After this first semester, you have begun the hard work of not just creating that voice but using it to teach, to guide, to shape young adults' lives. In the days ahead, as you begin to imagine the second semester, see yourself in June, looking back on all the months to come, your hands full of all you learned along the way, and see yourself as the teacher you dream of being and with faith, patience, and hard work will *become*.

Your colleague,

Jim

How do you organize time to make sure you get everything done?

Dear Joy:

The new semester seems to be off to a good beginning for you. You seem more relaxed. The spirit of your class seems healthy and happy enough. You can always tell the difference between a class kids are happy to come to and one they resent. I have been grateful for the chance to begin the second semester anew in my AP class; it's a chance to clear the board and, drawing on all I learned the first semester, play a better game.

Minutes into the second semester you feel the difference when it comes to time. Suddenly you realize this is the second half of the game and there is no overtime. You realize that the semester will be fragmented by holidays, interminable testing, Spring Break, and then the sudden slide toward the end of the year that makes time gallop all the harder. I mention this because it will help you immensely to create a schema—that is, a big picture—for the semester to make sure you have time to do what matters most. *What matters most*, of course, is a loaded phrase for many of us these days, as you can well appreciate when passing out the state test preparation materials the school purchased or giving your students the common assessment the district now requires in order to help teachers assess and better prepare students for the state tests in April.

Sad to say, any *real* substantial teaching you want to get in needs to be done by April fifteenth. Of course this is somewhat arbitrary, but not entirely. A few years ago I studied our school's use of time, itemizing *everything* that took instructional time away from me: assemblies, field trips, counselors coming in to use class time to plan for the next year, and so on. It gains momentum in the spring, further fracturing the instructional narrative line of the semester. Thus to plan ahead is to ensure more cohesion in the story the semester will tell through the work you have the kids do.

Of course we can *never* get it all done or done well enough. Teaching an English class is like putting one of those self-assemble furnishings together: You seem always, not matter how carefully, how precisely you follow the instructions, to have a mess of parts left over that you never found a way to include. So you put them in a bag, relegate them to that drawer where such scraps go, and keep an eye open for anything that reveals a need for additional support.

Still, I don't like to have my success as a teacher be accidental, so I keep tinkering to improve my efficiency and effectiveness. It's rather like some cyclist who tries first one thing and then another to see which one improves his speed or the handling of his bike. (Cycling is no doubt on my mind because I went for a wonderful ride late this afternoon that ended with a quick trip across the Golden Gate Bridge at sunset.) For me, this tinkering amounts to revising these instructional templates I have been playing with the last few years. The idea is to keep reflecting on the elements of an effective lesson plan but also the structure of the period in light of all that I need to accomplish; yet it's no success to say I merely "did" or "taught" something. To assign, as I have realized again and again this year, is not to teach. This first year of teaching this new course reminds me how much effort goes into simply figuring out the *what* (i.e., what I will have them read, what they will write, and so on); what time remains goes to figuring out the *how* (i.e., most appropriate instructional approach to that material). But it's now 7:49 on a Sunday evening and I have spent probably four hours today just searching for, evaluating, choosing, and formatting the materials I will use in class this week (for just that one class!). That was the *what;* the *why* is that this particular material is on the AP test and the kids are struggling with it. The instructional (lesson) template shown in Figure 14.1 serves as a defense against my lack of time to think about the *how* and thus ensures some reasonable level of cohesive, effective instruction.

Do I need only four inches at the bottom for my lesson plan? No! It comes with a blank side on the back to add more. Without boring you to death about this, let me just say what I was trying to accomplish with this tool and why I like it. First, the little Four Cs box in the upper corner serves as a sort of quick check to ensure I am hitting as many of the Cs as possible. If the lesson doesn't address commitment, what hope will I have of any success? This four-square box, though small, is mighty: it is like a compass representing the four corners of the globe to me as I chart our course for the period. I might not be able to fill in or check all four, but it reminds me at least to *try.*

The Academic Essentials, which are quickly listed below the Four Cs, remind me to use as many of these as possible to maximize comprehension and understanding but also to increase their capacities (e.g., speed, stamina, dexterity) and competencies (mental abilities and academic skills). These

C^1	C^2
C^3	C^4

Academic Essentials

- Read
- Write
- Talk
- Take notes
- Take tests

- Generate
- Evaluate
- Analyze
- Organize
- Synthesize

Class		Subject[1]
Period	Date	Subject[2]

Personal Curriculum	Public Curriculum

Notes

Before
- What do they already know?
- What do they need to learn?
- What instructional technique is best?
- What is their motivation for doing this?
- What is the Big Idea this relates to?
- What is the best instructional setup?
- Do they know what a successful performance of this task looks like?
- How will you know they achieved the desired outcome?
- Are there other ways students can demonstrate understanding or mastery?

During
- Is the instructional technique and/or academic strategy effective?
- Who is struggling and why? How can you help them?
- Are students making the expected progress toward the state's goals?
- How can you have them further manipulate the material to improve comprehension, fluency, and memory?

After
- What do you want them to do now?
- How can they demonstrate their understanding and ability?
- Did they reach the instructional goal?
- If not, what should you reteach and by what method to ensure improved learning, fluency, and memory?
- How can they extend what they learned here to improve fluency and memory?
- What do they need to do or learn next—and how does that relate to what they learned through this lesson?

Figure 14.1[1]

ten words serve as a sort of checklist to ensure I am not missing some opportunity to integrate another level of processing or skill development in my lesson. I find the five cognitive abilities—generate, evaluate, analyze, organize, and synthesize—especially useful when planning and teaching, as they provide a Cuisinart-like process that ensures kids use their minds in multiple ways to engage in authentic academic thinking.

The personal versus public distinction stems from kids' comments last semester (in the AP class) that I was overemphasizing the AP test at the expense of the more personal reasons we read literature. Without going into it here, this was a valid criticism about what is perhaps an inevitable pitfall for the new AP teacher with thirty-five kids, many of whom grow quite irritable if it is not clear how the current activity will lead to a higher score on the AP test. Some other time I will use a letter as a couch to discuss with you my ambivalence about this course that seems to value the ability to read poetry with the efficiency of a lawn mower, but not tonight. The point is that this latest lesson plan template has been helping me ensure that I make the personal connections and, moreover, balance these against the public (e.g., College Board, AP test) demands on me. It might seem a bit of an odd analogy, but when you are cutting wood on a table saw, it can be helpful to create what is called a stop or a block, which amounts to little more than a piece of wood clamped to the table saw to guarantee that each cut is the same size, a trick that raises the quality of your work.

Two other parts of the template bear explanation: the Subject[1] and Subject[2] boxes and the Before • During • After section.

The Subject boxes are meant to get me focused: what is the *subject* of this lesson? As if a lesson or class were an essay, the student (like a reader) wonders what the point is, the focus, the purpose. Every class is, after all, a rhetorical occasion, one built around not just a subject but the purpose we bring to that subject (e.g., persuade them of its importance, of the usefulness of a method, the quality of some text, author, or idea). Moreover, while the fifty or so pages of standards make us feel like we should be doing *everything* simultaneously (or we will never get it all in, get it all *taught*!), the truth is a class, like an essay, can sustain only one (at the most, two) main subjects, and even then, it needs a real organizational structure to bring some cohesion to the lesson. So these two Subject boxes help me by saying, *Hey, wait a minute: Before you go running off to make some lesson plan, think about what you are doing, what you will try to accomplish!* This makes sense when you compare it to writing: writers typically identify a subject, then figure out what they want to say about it, considering along the way the best genre, tone, diction, and organizational structure to use so they can achieve their rhetorical purpose with the reader.

Which brings us, finally, to the Before • During • After section. As the questions suggest, they are meant to help me stop and think at different phases of the instructional sequence about what I am trying to accomplish, the best way to accomplish that, and the means by which I will know if I *did* accomplish it. It is *not* meant to be a recipe, a formula for standardized lessons; rather these three stages are there, again, like the block on the table saw, to ensure some level of consistency, so that my success as a teacher one day does not seem like an accident I cannot knowingly repeat or amplify the next day. I can't afford for my or my students' success to be an accident, so this template keeps evolving as I study what works and what doesn't.

It's worth noting, perhaps, since I am talking so much about planning and organizing here, that I put this sheet (filled in, of course) with blank copies of any handouts, subsequent copies of student exemplars, transparencies we used, and so on—all that day's materials—in the master binder on my podium so when I revisit the material next year, I can find everything the way a writer might a draft and then set to revising the lesson. Of course some times the best revision is a recycling can or a fire, for by the time I return to this year's lessons next year, I will have made a year's worth of mistakes, will have learned a year's worth of lessons, and will better understand the material and can thus focus more deeply on the *how* instead of the *what* of the curriculum.

I might say that such a tool as this template is a way of making me smarter than I am on my own. As Donald Norman says in his wonderful book (books are tools, too!) *Things That Make Us Smart*: "The power of the unaided mind is highly overrated. Without external aids, memory, thought, and reasoning are all constrained. But human intelligence is highly flexible and adaptive, superb at inventing procedures and objects that overcome its own limits. The real powers come from devising external aids that enhance cognitive abilities."[1] At the risk of sounding too essay-like, I will share one last passage, which appears at the end of Norman's classic book:

> The calculator is an excellent example of a complementary technology, one that supports our abilities but does not get in the way. Want other examples? The book. Writing in general. Or how about tools that have evolved to fit the true needs of the user, tools that have resulted from years of shaping by individual craftspeople? Such examples include tools for carpentry and metalworking, tools for the farm and garden, for camping and mountain climbing, art and cooking. But to find the good tools,

the ones as yet unblemished by fads or the need to put appearance before function, you must visit the stores for professionals: a professional restaurant supplies store, a good old-fashioned hardware store, or a hiking and camping store. Here you can find tools that have slowly evolved over years to fit the needs of the people and the task.

I love making tools, Joy, and I suppose my enthusiasm about it spilled over into this letter. I grew up in the garage with my dad and tools, building things from his scraps, and now those tools sleep in my garage, my father's hands stilled, but my head filled with all the knowledge he gave me about the beauty and use of tools, especially those we create for ourselves to solve the problems we encounter in whatever work is ours. My father spent thirty-eight years making books and working in the printing business. My work now is to make tools to help kids read the books people like my father produce. By way of closing, I will offer this poem by Gary Snyder, a favorite, which brings some poetic conclusion to what I have discussed here:

AXE HANDLES

One afternoon the last week in April
Showing Kai how to throw a hatchet
One-half turn and it sticks in a stump.
He recalls the hatchet-head
Without a handle, in the shop
And go gets it, and wants it for his own.
A broken-off axe handle behind the door
Is long enough for a hatchet,
We cut it to length and take it
With the hatchet head
And working hatchet, to the wood block.
There I begin to shape the old handle
With the hatchet, and the phrase
First learned from Ezra Pound
Rings in my ears!
"When making an axe handle
the pattern is not far off."
And I say this to Kai
"Look: We'll shape the handle
By checking the handle
Of the axe we cut with—"
And he sees. And I hear it again:

It's in Lu Ji's Wen Fu, fourth century
A.D. "Essay on Literature"—in the
Preface: "In making the handle of an axe
By cutting wood with an axe
The model is indeed near at hand."
My teacher Shih-hsiang Chen
Translated that and taught it years ago
And I see: Pound was an axe,
Chen was an axe, I am an axe
And my son a handle, soon
To be shaping again, model
And tool, craft of culture,
How we go on.[2]

Enjoy the week ahead, Joy. That's what it's there for.

Your colleague,

Jim

Interlude 4
AN EXCHANGE OF LETTERS ABOUT
THE HARD WORK OF IMPROVING

⌒

Dear Joy:

I thought you might find the following exchange of some interest. It is too late to say much else other than that I am not sure I should give this to him—but know I will. As we have discussed on numerous occasions, people often fail to recognize and honor how much time it takes to get good at something, that wanting a successful result is not enough, especially if you are not willing to do the work that leads to such success. As Colin Powell said at some point, success is never an accident. Nor, I would add, is it a birthright or a gene. To quote the poet Jack Gilbert, "it is the normal excellence of long achievement," which is to say the long steady effort that culminates in the excellence we seek, even as the game changes and we must set off and begin anew. So it is with learning and students, so it is with teaching and teachers.

Enjoy the weekend.

Jim

~ ~

Dear Mr. Burke,

After receiving the compare/contrast essay back today about the Dickenson and Frost's poem, I can't help but feel exceedingly more discouraged by your class. I received a four on that essay, a D; or in other words, an essay that was below average. It is not so much as the grade I received on the essay, than me seeing no difference in the essay I received a D on, and the essay I received an A– on (the *Crime and Punishment* essay for the final). I reviewed each, as well as the AP English Literature 2004 guidelines, and feel that the grades assigned do not fit the scoring rubric. I do not feel that in my compare/contrast essay I "misread the poems," "[failed] to develop a coherent basis for comparing/contrasting the two poems," or "[relied] completely on paraphrase." I don't believe I had "inadequate" evidence, "an accumulation of errors," or a "focus that is unclear . . ." On the other hand, I did feel as if I followed similar directions to your "AP compare/contrast poems essay wizard" when I wrote that essay.

Please do not take this as if I am criticizing you as a teacher, I am just expressing my frustration and confusion about AP English.

I just don't understand how someone can become a better writer by reading essays that are considered "good," trying to follow an outline yet not expressing a formulaic type of writing, and striving from a thesis to show something else. I do not feel as if you should "hold my hand," when it comes to writing, yet I don't think I am getting any better as a writer with the path I am taking now. I really am trying to learn how to write better, yet I don't see how someone can judge an essay to be "bad" or "good." I can understand how someone can prove a thesis, thus making their essay "good," but other than that, I am not sure.

I feel as if I am trying hard and getting nowhere, and often don't understand the reasons for many of the exercises we do in class.

And honestly, I'm a bit scared about sending this to you. I don't know how you will react.

Once again, please do not take this as if I am criticizing your teaching methods or just expressing my anger over getting a bad grade on an essay. Also don't think that I don't try when it comes to English, and am just whining. When it comes down to everything, I simply want to become a better writer, and am unsure what that really is.

Thanks.

Greg Lee

~ ~

February 11, 2005

Dear Greg:

It's late (11:30) and there are other things I should do, but your letter asks important questions that make the other things I should be doing seem less urgent at the moment. Again, let me reiterate my appreciation for your letter. We get much more in return when we enter into conversations in good faith, asking honest questions about subjects that matter to us. I have had other students, this year even, who took a very different approach and such letters only end the conversation the student hopes to begin.

You raise a few different subjects: writing, assessing, teaching, learning, and reading. I'll do what I can to address these in ways that can enlighten us both in ways that make a difference. Unless I indicate otherwise, I am speaking about students in general, not you in particular.

I'd prefer to work backwards, starting with reading. There is an inevitable and complex relationship between reading and writing in this class: people can't write too well about texts they don't understand beyond the obvious surface details. Frankly, many need to improve their ability to read with precision; they too often leave the text behind and engage in private readings, which they believe are correct despite their lack of evidence from the text. People in this class must be able to read both with and *against* the grain, on and below the surface. These are very complicated forms of reading that demand that the student read not only for literal and figurative meaning, but also for the purpose of writing an insightful analysis of the meaning, purpose, and effect. Such reading requires patience, commitment, and knowledge—of literary texts, ideas, the world, language, religion. I'm sometimes surprised by what kids don't know, to be honest. So I keep trying to figure out ways to bridge those gaps, to help people without, as you say, "holding their hand." In an ideal world, an AP lit class should have about 15–20 kids, much more of a seminar format; I do my best with what I have. But I'm rarely satisfied with myself.

As for learning, we might borrow a line from the poet we read this week: Roethke. He said, "I take my learning slow, learning by going where it is I have to go." One thing that complicates (or should it clarify?) the notion of "learning" in the class is the purpose of the course. I think we all (I will generalize) suffer from a certain schism: on the one hand we want to engage in thoughtful discussions about literature and ideas and better understand our place in the world, or the world within us; on the other hand, however, everyone wants to do well on the AP test and so filters everything (or so it sometimes seems) through the one blunt question: How will this help me get a passing score on the AP test? And if it won't, why the heck are we doing it? While it's discouraging to read that you "often don't understand the reasons for many of the exercises we do in class," I accept your comment as true for you and no doubt for some others, since no one is ever the only one who has such feelings or questions. The best answer I can give you is that I always have a reason, based on sound research, for what I do; but I also scrutinize myself and the results pretty closely to see if what I do is effective, if it makes the difference I thought it would. If it doesn't, I refine the method or toss it out; this is why I appreciate your comments and listen to you: like you, I'm just trying to get better.

Thus one question you might ask yourself—I don't say this to be critical or challenge you—is to ask what efforts you have made to improve your own learning, your own performance, and what difference those efforts have made. Those kids who have excelled, for example, routinely speak of trying new things and examining what kind of difference these efforts made. They develop their own individual strategies by studying their performance and learning what helps them perform well. Again, this takes real time and commitment to one's learning. We should only do what makes a difference, the tricky piece for me, of course, being that no one technique makes a difference with all 33 kids in any one class. The feedback I sought the other day on that writing technique, for example, had about 18 people saying it "really helped," 7 saying it helped a bit, and the rest saying it served no point. That was from second period; so I made small but effective adjustments when I used the technique in third period (yours). Again, reading through the different comments, I found about the same breakdown. What one student thinks is very helpful another thinks is pointless. In the end, I can only go by what proves most effective.

I suspect the sequence we did this week will prove effective: time on Monday to try a timed reading and beginning as if for an AP test. Just enough time to create a start. But then time to refine it, see how others approached the same problem (i.e., reading and responding to the text). Then time to go home and think, reread, consider others' claims, and use all that new insight to refine your own reading and, I hope, writing performance in the comfort of your own home. Then the opportunity to respond, get feedback that you can then use to further refine. Then today: analyze the structure, the design of your writing (focus, organization, development = FOD) to help you assess the extent to which it is balanced in these three crucial areas. Several mentioned how helpful they found today's discussion about FOD; a couple others said the flower diagram was useful. Others, perhaps you among them, no doubt found none of that helpful. And here, at this hour, I try to pick up one more run in the game, here in the bottom of the eleventh, after everyone has gone home: just you and me out on the diamond, me trying to find one more way to help you see what each must find for himself. But what is effective if this, in the big picture, prepares you only for a timed writing test called the AP exam?

Thus we return to the bigger picture of assessing and writing, two issues at the heart of your letter and frustration. As for the rubric: I find many students have little sense of the quality of writing—their own or others'. What I have tried to do by using examples in class—"I just don't understand how someone can become a better writer by reading essays that are considered 'good'"—is to get you guys to internalize the language structures, the precision of analysis that appears in these successful essays. Perhaps the best example of the difference this can make is the number of comments I had this week from people about the sample opening of *your* essay, which I included in that sheet I created. (A sheet like that, for the record, is the result of about five hours of work). This is actually not unrelated to my point: the five hours I spend on such a page is a measure of my commitment to the craft of teaching. I might not get it right (indeed, that is why my first question after using it with you was "How can I improve it?" "Did it help?") but this is what it takes to work toward the kind of result I seek. When you read a truly effective piece of writing, you have the feeling that each word, every sentence was individually polished, set like a gem in that particular place to serve a specific purpose. That writer knows what he or she wants to say, has some clear idea in their own mind that comes from a deep insight into that text that came from patient, diligent reading.

Again, I don't doubt you when you say you are trying hard; I know you are. And if you feel like the score on the latest essay (Dickinson/Frost) was unfair, let's sit down and discuss it so you can understand why I thought as I did and I can, if I'm wrong, make the necessary changes. The question remains, however, whether the effort you make is the right one. What do you do, for example, to make better sense of those poems this week? Going over the test today with people, I felt all the more convinced that they had been lazy, impatient, imprecise readers (I realize it's timed, rushed) who either ask no questions or ask the wrong questions, or ask the right questions but at the wrong time; thus they have no effect. I wonder, for example, how many people will consult the dictionary when reading the poems this week—a *good* dictionary, one with etymologies in it, for this is the level of precision that a student must bring to the work if he or she is to reach that level of consistency. I can't emphasize this enough: the difference between being able to write in general, and being prepared/able to write with great effect about a text they have to read and interpret. Many—*many*—in the class seem to focus on what they can do, what they are capable of doing instead of looking at what they did and making effective decisions that lead to a different result. Some have sent me papers as emails or met with me at brunch; and I see their writing getting better, in part, because I see their reading improving as they use the strategies we discuss.

It's nearly one, so I need to bring this letter to a close. But here is my point, Greg: You have to ask yourself, honestly, what you are doing or have done that leads you to expect to improve. You should be able to point to specific things you have done. I can say, for example, that I listened to you, that I took your invitation to think about our class, my teaching, and tried to think out loud about what works and what doesn't instead of defending myself, instead of assuming I am a final draft as a teacher. I think many have a difficult time accepting how hard it is, how much time it takes, to get very good at something; so much fumbling forward leaves us feeling frustrated, a feeling we resent without understanding how inevitable it is. We too often want to go straight to great without first learning how to be good. You took the risk of honesty with me; I'll trust you as much: I'm not a great AP English teacher—yet. I have to learn how the course works first, like the mountain climber who makes his initial ascent and learns first what *doesn't* work, what *isn't* possible, en route to learning what does work, what is possible; then, like Emily Dickinson, we grow "accustomed" to what was unfamiliar. What I can assure you of, Greg, is that no mistake I make is intentional; that the same frustrations you feel at not achieving a sense of consistent excellence and success on your papers is what I feel with my own teaching. Yet this part of the process is inevitable for us; and the only solution is to not shy away from the hard work, the complexity of the craft of teaching or writing, and to move forward confident that we will both improve if we work at it, and work in ways that make a difference—the kind of difference I hope a letter like this makes for you.

Thank you for the invitation to think so long and so deeply about the work I love so much.

Sincerely,

Mr. Burke

P.S.: While there is nothing overtly personal or otherwise embarrassing in this letter, I would ask that you not let others read it as it was written to you with the understanding that it was a private letter. Thank you for respecting my privacy in this respect.

P.P.S.: Here it is, one in the morning again, and back to my thoughts in response to your letter, Greg. I've spoken a lot about effort, about the long commitment required of getting better, of doing what makes a difference. I've thumbed through the pile of essays from class today, the ones we spent all week on. It seems worth noting that while the papers of those who sit around you have multiple drafts and show evidence of using some of the techniques I discussed this week, your paper written on Monday the 7th remains a slightly altered draft with about ten words crossed out. It is a good beginning, the kind of thing people were supposed to spend the week improving upon. It's what Duncan has, for example, as the first of three drafts; his subsequent drafts show precise, deliberate efforts that steadily improved the paper because they led not only to improved writing but improved understanding of the poems themselves, which subsequently further improved the essay.

So I end our written conversation here by reminding you that what makes the biggest difference is the effort you invest in your own growth, the extent to which you accept responsibility for your own learning. It might seem a random comparison, but to become one of the better tennis players in the state as a kid, I hit backhand slices down the line for hours; then worked on perfecting a certain serve, and so on, crafting my game through hours of playing, coaching, analyzing, practicing, and performing. I did equivalent exercises with writing when I began to get serious about improving my writing skills. But we don't get better by just writing; we get better by investing the full measure of our intelligence into the study of each performance, focusing on what works and what doesn't. The reason I can justify spending a couple hours on this letter to you is that I know, from years of experience, that such an effort makes a difference, and so it is worth the time—because *you* are worth that time. The question I end with is this: Are you investing the same kind of time and energy into getting great, and if so, how does this week's performance on the Roethke poem show that?

Dear Joy:

I owe you an end to the story of the exchange with that boy I included in the last letter. I did not send the letter when I finished it. I have a history of dashing off letters, well-written, powerful letters—to students, principals, teachers, even superintendents—that I should have known not to send . . . but sent anyway. I was also somewhat anxious because Greg, the young man to whom I wrote the letter, is close friends with a boy I had some troubles with last semester; I would have felt too vulnerable if Greg had showed him that letter. But I wrote the letter in good faith, wrote it not to share with you, not as a mere exercise in personal and professional reflection; heck, if I reflected any more than I already do I'd probably turn into a mirror. But when I saw his paper from this week, I knew I had to send the letter and add a postscript. It was too important, the opportunity was there: it's what I became a teacher for, after all, isn't it? This is the deep work of teaching: it is where we can matter most, make the biggest difference. And, sadly, it is precisely what many teachers feel they no longer have time for as they feel compelled to focus only on test scores, which often come at the cost of such essential mentoring conversations.

So I sent the letter—for Greg, foremost, because I care about him and know he has some troubles at home that leave him in need of men to help him trust in who he is and guide him to be who he wants to be. But I also sent it for me, for *us* (i.e., teachers), as almost a conscious act of rebellion against the constraints society wants to put on me and my work. It's what I came into teaching to do, to be: a teacher who spends his passion on the subject matter and craft of teaching as much as he does on the kids in his care, whom he hopes to shape through that teaching, those stories, that craft. This is precisely what Louise Rosenblatt, one of the truly *great* minds and voices in our profession—who, as it happens, died this week at *one hundred*, just as her last book, written when she was one hundred, was being published—meant when she wrote in *Literature as Exploration*, "The teacher will do neither literature nor students a service if he tries to evade ethical issues. He will be exerting some kind of influence, positive or nega-

110

tive, through his success or failure in helping the student develop habits of thoughtful ethical judgment. The teacher should scrutinize his own ethical criteria, which must color anything that he says or does in the classroom. . . . The literature classroom can stimulate the students themselves to develop a thoughtful approach to human behavior."[1]

I sent it off (by email) at about one in the morning, going to sleep satisfied with the work I had done, grateful for the delicious dinner and good conversation with my wife earlier that evening at a little Japanese restaurant in our neighborhood. And when I woke six hours later, Greg's response was waiting for me as the reward for my decision to take the risk:

> Mr. Burke,
>
> Thank you very much for your letter. I really appreciate you taking time out of your hectic schedule to respond to me. Your letter actually did help me a lot, in more of a way than you might have expected; you've given me a lot to think about. I cannot stress how much I appreciate everything you've done for me, as well as the time and enthusiasm you put into class each day. I am glad that I read your letter, and it gives me motivation to take all the in-class assignments more seriously, instead of dismissing some of them as unhelpful and doing a second-rate job on them.
>
> As I skim back through your letter I can't imagine how hard your job must be, really. I'm not sure what else to say except thanks for everything. Thanks for showing me the insight of a teacher—I'll never look at another one the same.
>
> Greg Lee
>
> P.S.: Do not worry about me keeping this conversation private.

Our role as mentors must never be compromised, something politicians and others sometimes lose sight of in the blizzard of their legislation and commentary. But kids need to find their way to the person they will listen to. Kids who are involved in other ethical institutions—church, community service groups, or even sports teams run by great coaches—have access to a wider pool of mentors to draw from, but many have only school and the hope of some teacher. Of course with thirty-five kids in a class, we cannot play this role for all our kids, but we can watch out for the one, like Greg, who rises to the top, who speaks up and reaches out, who extends the invitation to himself as much as to us. Kids need us more than society wants to admit; and you, as a new teacher, are a crucial part of our profession's story, for you must be able to be the teacher you wanted to be when you entered the profession, must know that this is part of the tradition of influence you have joined.

Such relationships, if they are truly mentoring relationships, do not stop when the school day ends or the curtain comes down on a year. The same day I got the letter from Greg this week, I received a letter from Nelson, a boy I taught as a freshman five years ago, whose parents brought him here years ago from Central America, chasing the dream we hope will come true for all our students. But they didn't know how school works, how kids get to college, how to help him with his studies. And Nelson, who only this month began attending a four-year college (after working at a sporting goods store to save up money during the fall semester), finds himself feeling not unlike Greg, the only difference being that he is on a huge college campus, in a new city, far from home. So he wrote to me, as he did so many times after that freshman year ended years ago, paying me the ultimate compliment of breaking all written conventions as, what, a show of familiarity, intimacy?

hey mr burke

its nelson again. just sending you an email to update you on how im doin here in long beach. the classes im taking right now are early american history (great teacher really funny guy), Public Speaking (really fun class), Criminal Justice in American society (the teacher is great and very interesting) and then i have chicano latino studies which is english class with a differnt name. this teacher im not so sure about. (you might know her Gladys Garcia she said she knows faculty at bhs). not only is she confusing as hell because her instructions are rarely clear but when we start asking questions she tells us we're all damaged because our parents raised us [on] tv and we now have attention spans the length of commercials. shes also frustrating because she isnt very helpful but also very picky. i havnt had an english teacher who cared about an essay more than its spelling and content since your english class. last draft i brought in she took 2 seconds to look at my paper told me my thesis was very vague. she wrote it down on my paper and that was all. when i asked her what i should do to make it better she told me to "focus" more. i thought before i knew what a thesis was now im not even sure how to write one or know how one looks like. i know its not high school, but she's not the biggest help so far. i have only had a few classes with her and rather not jump to conclusions but so far her class is more frustrating than helpful. other than that i have been doing good. i might go and volunteer with the california state alcoholic beverage control. they're looking for underage students who want to help by acting as a regular person who wants to buy alcohol but is underage. they want minorities under the age of 20 who is interested in this field of work which is me! haha i cant think of anything better of being the main person who took down some bad guys. yea im pretty excited about it and ill update you on how that goes. well mr. burke im off to work on my horrible essay as mrs. garcia probably would say. tell me how your book is going and how you been

Still your student,
nelson

In the storm of the days and years ahead, we must tie ourselves to something we can believe in, something that will help us understand not only our work but ourselves, our profession, and the tradition of which we are both a part. In the old days on the plains, farmers would tie a long rope around their waist and lash it to their barn door as they set off into the blizzard to retrieve their stray cattle, who would otherwise perish. The rope was a defense against getting lost themselves, for the plains of the past were littered with the bodies of both the cattle and the men who got lost trying to find them. I know who I am when I get a letter from Nelson and a letter from Greg; I know my purpose. Tying myself to the door of these values, these core principles of commitment to teaching and to mentoring, I head out into the storm not to find these boys, but rather to keep doing the work of helping them find themselves, but letting them, if they wish, tie their rope to me as they head into the sound and fury of their own life, so they can find their way back to ask advice or just tell me they are "doing good," as Nelson says.

I can't thank you enough for giving me cause to think about these issues. These letters are part of the rope that keeps me anchored even as the wind of it all whips past my bright red ears.

Your colleague,

Jim

Interlude 5
SEXUAL ABUSE

⌒

Jim:

I am moved by the situation/letter you shared with me and your student. My mind is filled with so many thoughts—so many "to do" lists. Yes I am captured by the enormous contrast between your situation (its success in revealing the power of a fabulous teacher) and a situation I just learned of that occurred at my own high school (it seems so long ago that I was there!). A twenty-five-year-old choir teacher was arrested last Tuesday for having a two-month relationship with one of his sixteen-year-old students. Oh the power of the teacher! I am told he was a dynamic musician and teacher and yet he has ruined his career and in the process has not only brought a girl down with him but the students who looked up to him. Not only is this girl, this child, and other children impacted by this situation, but the school and the community are now reminded how the world/school is not always a safe place. This situation brings me down and reminds me of the power of my situation as a teacher—the power to be a mentor and a positive influence—and reminds me of how careful one must be to never let any impropriety creep into one of the most amazing professions anyone could be a part of. I will not be one to bring down my profession as this man has. I aspire to be like you, a teacher who upholds the profession, our profession, to be what it truly was meant to be . . .

Joy

Why would a teacher have a relationship with a student and thus harm not only the student but himself?

Dear Joy:

From the moment I entered teaching I have heard horror stories like the one you told in your last letter. When I was getting my teaching credential, I had Dr. House, a pleasant man with a nice smile who had been out of the classroom since the year I was born: 1961. The one legacy of his teaching is a tendency I have to reflect on my work by writing about it. He had us keep journals about our student teaching; he also had us bring in articles from the newspapers about teaching. And we always talked about the dangers of the student-teacher relationship (as he saw them). Ours was an unusual class: about 80 percent men. So Dr. House took this as an invitation to concentrate on the very issue you raise in your letter: boundaries as they relate to the student-teacher relationship. Every week we heard a different story about some teacher who got in trouble. Sometimes they initiated it, other times they were the victim of some accusation that was ultimately dismissed, but only after much pain and, at times, unjust punishment.

The worst story he told—we actually read an article about it—involved a much-beloved music teacher who had been a model citizen and a mentor to decades of students in his community. He taught them everything, staying with them after school, going to their homes for private lessons. Then, when he was about sixty-three, a young girl said he had touched her. And he had: just as he had done for decades, tapping students on their knee to help them feel the rhythm they struggled to catch. On this particular day, perhaps because he was tired, or getting old—who knows—his hand sort of fumbled on her knee instead of making the crisp tap he usually made. He immediately apologized, saying, "I'm sorry, Janice, that wasn't appropriate." Later, her mother asked her if everything was going well with the lessons. She mentioned to her mother the incident that afternoon. The mother accused him of molesting her daughter. He lost his job. His wife of thirty-five years divorced him. His kids wouldn't talk to him. (This all happened in a hurricane of weeks.) He went to jail while he awaited trial. He suffered a mental breakdown and had to be institutionalized. He lost all his money.

And when it was too late, the truth came out: The girl had never wanted to have music lessons, had *hated* the idea, but her mother had insisted. So when this incident arose, the girl thought she saw a way to get out of doing the lessons. Then when everything spun out of control, she felt too ashamed to admit that he had not molested her; she probably didn't want to look bad!

This is, of course, different than the story you tell of a teacher knowingly entering into a sexual relationship with a student. I think it must be all the more upsetting that it should happen at your own alma mater. I had something similar happen, but in some ways it was worse. When I graduated from high school, I went on one of those European trips with about sixty other kids and adult advisors. One of the advisors, the head of the program actually, was the head counselor at my high school. When we were traveling around Europe we saw him act like a moron, often embarrassing himself with drink, but never saw anything *wrong*. Then we came back home, and one morning the newspaper ran an article about him, saying he was being charged with about forty counts of statutory rape for an ongoing relationship with a girl he'd met on one of the Europe trips the summer before. I was stunned, but it also made me look at what he had said and how he had acted in an entirely new light, and it made me also realize how naïve, even at eighteen, kids are. They are so busy thinking they know what's going on that they often don't notice what's really going on—until it's too late.

The whole situation has become much more bizarre in the last few years with that middle school teacher who fell in love with and had children by her seventh-grade student despite the fact that she was married and had three kids of her own already. Prison seems to have done little to put out the fire, and so now, five years later, she is out and they are no doubt together, offering our twisted society some strange variation on its favorite love story: *Romeo and Juliet*.

All of this brings us back to the central theme of our conversation, not just in this letter but all of them: the power of the teacher. Ours is, in its own way, sacred work. The theologian Matthew Fox, writing about work, said, "The young need elders and mentors; they need healthy adults around them."[1] The key word here is, of course, *healthy*. In the last few years we have heard so much about the scandals of priests, and sometimes coaches, who were abusing children. Yet at the heart of all these stories is the essential truth that Fox mentions: kids need adult guides to help them find their way through the wilderness within them and also the one around them. This makes our work inevitably intimate and powerful in ways that most people understand but also mistrust, especially if you are a man. In a profession that is approximately 80 percent women, people wonder why men would choose to work with kids, especially elementary kids. And then out of the other side of their mouth, they bemoan the trouble kids get into because they lack male role models and guidance.

There is nothing as wonderful and scary as the feeling of trust a kid puts in your hands when, for whatever reason, they choose you as their Teacher, the one they will give themselves permission to listen to, to emulate, to follow. There is such a depth of trust that it can blind both the child and the adult, confusing the roles, the responsibilities. At some very deep and meaningful level, that student has given themselves over to you to help them create themselves. I can't imagine rejecting that trust, that faith, out of fear, but some do. So I do my best to maintain boundaries while at the same time doing the work I chose: helping kids become successful, happy adults. Alice Walker said it better than I can: "Good teachers bring us to life. Literally. It's as if they take us by the hand when we are unsure of just what life is, and they lead us to the fullness and beauty of what it means to be alive. I think the Latin *educare* means to bring out into the light."[2] And William Ayers, in his book *To Teach: The Journey of a Teacher*, adds: "The work of a teacher—exhausting, complex, idiosyncratic, never twice the same—is at its heart, an intellectual and ethical enterprise. Teaching is the vocation of vocations, a calling that shepherds a multitude of other callings. It is an activity that is intensely practical and yet transcendent, brutally matter-of-fact, and yet fundamentally a creative act. Teaching begins in challenge and is never far from mystery."[3]

It is this challenge that Ayers speaks of, this "bringing out into the light" that Walker refers to, that makes our work so powerful and, in the hands of the wrong person, so dangerous. I didn't enter the profession to grade papers all day (as I have for the last twelve hours), though I find the hard work of teaching kids to write satisfying. I didn't enter the profession to help the school get higher scores on the state tests, though I accept responsibility for my part of that work, tiresome as it may be. I think Ayers captures it pretty well in his quotation above.

So what, then, do I do? How do I manage my relationship, maintain my power to help and heal without using it in any way to hurt? I trust in the kids but am not reckless or naïve. Thus I will meet with a boy or girl at lunch in my room to go over their essay, discuss grades, help them with assignments. When I do this I am rarely alone, since other kids tend to gather in the room when I am there. If there weren't anyone else in my room, I would still meet with the kid—*unless* for any reason I felt awkward or otherwise unsafe. Then, without making a big deal about it, I might say, "It would be a lot easier for me if we met in the library today. Can you meet me there?" Then I would be around people. And I write notes to kids but always keeping in mind how others might interpret them. I do this for the simple reason that kids, girls included, have told me over the years of the difference these letters or notes made. Many of them have the notes—usually dashed off on index cards and passed to the student when they left—tacked to their bulletin boards in their rooms (as they or parents have told me). I like writing the notes for the very reason that the kids can have them to read and reread, so they can hear my words over and over. And email now brings a new level of communication that we must learn to master. Here, for example, is a brief exchange between me and Karina, a wonderful senior who has allowed me to challenge her, help her—who wants to get better at everything. She puts a lot of power into my hands. Karina was out for the day, so she wrote me.

From: Karina Edwards (Student)

Subject: My absence

Hey Mr. Burke,

I am emailing you to find out what I need to [do] tonight on the rough draft I wrote last night regarding Owens' and Komunyakaa's poems.

Sorry for missing today, but this morning I woke up with a horrible migraine.

If you could email me at your convenience I would greatly appreciate it.

Thank you,

Karina Edwards

P.S.: I would also like to commend you on your teaching techniques, preparing us for the AP exam. I thoroughly enjoy reading and analyzing poetry. I also feel like the exercises we do are very helpful and I feel as though my writing skills continue to show signs of improvement (or at least I feel more confident in my writing).

~~~~~~

I feel great empathy, Miss Edwards: I had, not a migraine, but an unusually tenacious headache for about 12 hours yesterday and it was not fun and certainly affected my productivity. As for HW: Take the draft essay you wrote last night and reread it, asking at every step the following of any claim, subclaim, or observation you make: How does this (e.g., the author's use of dehumanizing images of war) contribute to the meaning of the text and the author's purpose and your claim about those?

We talked briefly today about these questions as tools to get everyone to think in more structured, consistent ways at that next level of insight. Your PS comments meant a great deal, Miss Edwards.[4] You are a model to us all, myself included, of diligence in the great effort to improve, which is all anyone can ever ask of us or we can ask of ourselves. We took a practice test today then read the play, so you can make those up.

Thanks for writing and for all your contributions to the class. We notice when you are not there. A little less light and energy in the room. Hope you feel better.

Mr. Burke

No doubt some would tell me I shouldn't say anything so personal or poetic as "a little less light and energy in the room," but we must all negotiate the terms of our vocation. I have written such notes to students for fifteen years now and never had one moment of fear, accusation, or doubt. Being a teacher is so much more than many realize and want to accept. I think this is especially true of English teachers, for we handle the language, the stories of people's lives. Without meaning any disrespect to other colleagues, you often hear people recall an English teacher with some special fondness, and when asked to explain they will say things like, "She taught me how to write," or "He taught us to love poetry," but what they are really saying is that these people gave them their voice, helped them find their best self, made their life a story they wanted to go out and tell, armed with all that the teacher had given them. It is not so different from the relationship that grows up between players and coaches. Vince Lombardi, the great football coach, made his team men during the process of making them into players. He said, "The quality of a person's life is in direct proportion to their commitment to excellence, regardless of their chosen field of endeavor." Well, you and I, Joy, have chosen teaching, education, English as our "field of endeavor." It's hard work: All good and important work is. And it's our work, work that has chosen us as much as we have chosen it. You end your letter saying, "I will not be one to bring down my profession as this man has. I aspire to . . . [uphold] the profession, our profession, to be what it truly was meant to be." The phrase I love most, so small but so deli-cious, is "our profession," for you are one of us, are inside this work now, and are moving into the deeper waters where the treasure is as large as the waters are deep.

Your colleague,

Jim

Question 17

What is the teacher's role when there is a crisis in the classroom?

⮬

Dear Joy:

I was reminded again of the deeper purpose of our work this morning when they told me one of my students nearly died in a terrible accident last night. At such moments, when a student everyone knows and cares about has died or hangs in the balance as Alyssa does now, we become for the students like news anchors for the country during times of national crisis. In another era, perhaps an era so long ago that it never really existed, when we imagine everyone gathered at church, ministers or priests, pastors or elders would have brought people together to pray, but schools—counselors and teachers, to be more specific—must often play this role today.

One of my students, a young woman with everything going for her—she's sitting on a heap of athletic scholarship offers, is a great student enrolled in advanced classes, has her peers' respect, and is beautiful—got cut off while driving home last night and rolled her car three times in the rain at high speeds. I knew something was wrong this morning at the faculty meeting when one of the counselors said, "I need to talk to Alyssa G—'s teachers." This is like when they "interrupt this show to bring you a special bulletin": it can only be bad news.

My immediate thought was that both of my senior classes were filled with close friends—running mates, lifelong friends—of Alyssa's. News like this, particularly in the digital age, spreads fast but not always accurately. So I began class by telling them what happened, what I knew. You realize at such times that you must be the one to be strong, to convey faith that things will be fine. Kids who felt like adults when they went to bed woke to such news only to feel the kid they are: vulnerable, mortal, scared, as if such events, such traumas violated the conventions of the story they thought they were living.

I am not one to encourage prayer in any public way. Still, it was ironic and sad when, driving home today after hearing the news of Alyssa's accident, knowing she was in the operating room all morning having a blood clot removed from her broken spine, I heard them discuss the Supreme Court's hearings today about the role of prayer in our lives. They kept saying that prayer had long ago been banned from the schools, and while I understand this, you wonder what that leaves you on a day like today. So I simply asked everyone in my classes to keep thinking about Alyssa, all day, and to send their thoughts her way.

I have not been in this mode of tending to kids in their grief and shock for about five years; indeed, I should say that the kids today were not actually so upset but seemed instead hunkered down against any possibility that they could lose their friend, their classmate, their peer. It is out of this kettle of fear that the most difficult emotions come in the event that things go badly.

I learned about this fear five years ago when a student of mine died in a terrible car accident two weeks before school ended. Mikey K, a wild, wonderful, chaotic bundle of distraction and joy, drove his car into a freeway divider (which I pass every morning on my way to work) at (the police estimated) ninety miles an hour. Only days before, he had stood before our sixth-period class, telling us his life story as part of a project. I had been thinking just that morning that this sixth-period class was more of a family than any I had ever known. I think I have mentioned them in other letters, but the point was that I realized they would need everything I could muster when they heard the news. As I was thinking about how to handle it, what to say to this class (I had heard about the accident during fifth period, right after lunch), which included his best friend and the girlfriend he was in a hurry to pick up that morning, I heard the public address system crackle on. I started to say, "Oh no, you're not going to just blurt out to the whole school . . ." when the principal announced, without getting the staff prepared in any way, "We are sorry to inform you that sophomore Mikey K— passed away this morning in a car accident." Coming as it did, from a voice over the loudspeaker, at the end of the year, without any warning, the news completely unhinged my kids.

We did many things that week to help the kids. The point I am trying to make, but am not doing so well, is that our work involves so much more than the report cards I turned in yesterday or the scores on state tests we discussed for two hours this morning. After telling the kids about Alyssa's accident, I passed out the AP practice test I had prepared for the day. And while it seemed pointless, even insensitive, my role was to help them move ahead, to keep them busy while the doctors did what they could to heal her. We moved from that into a discussion of the three phases of life—orientation, disorientation, and new orientation—relating it to *Heart of Darkness* and their own lives as seniors, but all the while I could only think of how much it related to Alyssa, who had suddenly entered into a phase of violent disorientation that will take her some years to work through.

I am uncomfortable pairing Mikey's death with Alyssa's accident for the obvious reason that she will survive and eventually tell this story to her children in years to come. But in this era when so many want to define the teacher as a mere delivery system, when they want to deny or at least ignore the sacred role we play in the community of our country's youth, I feel compelled to bring attention to this part of our work, to remind you that right alongside the standards for grammar or reading stand the standards of compassion and modeling for kids the responsibility adults must be ready to assume. When Mikey passed away, the kids lacked the language with which to discuss the event or make sense of it. I realized, in the midst of the trauma, as we prepared for a candle light vigil on the school's front lawn, that I still had his final paper in my bag, ungraded. I knew what it said because he had already delivered it to the class. Instead of writing something to speak at the vigil, I used his own words, arranging them into a poem (from his prose) so that he might speak to us in his own voice:

THE UNFINISHED SYMPHONY OF MICHAEL K—

As a young boy
my life was a calm flowing
stream with clear, blue waters.
It has become a waterfall
crying to see the light
of those friends I will never forget.

My mom said I always tried to imitate
my sister on the piano
Little did I know that playing
the piano was a talent
God gave me. A love
for the piano will always burn
inside me.

The halls were so big.
I felt so small, so helpless, I guess.

I came from a little Armenian school.
By June I was pretty well known
and had a gorgeous girlfriend.
It was perfect.

I am lost now, but in a different way.
I have changed. I am smarter.
Only the people I trust see
"the True me."

I am still a teenager.
I am still learning.
I will be learning
my whole life through.

My music would carry me to heaven.

I read this poem, Mikey's words, on a warm June evening, by the light of candles and a television camera to a couple hundred people gathered under the massive oak trees on our school's front lawn. I'm sure I had piles of finals to score, and the other myriad tasks to tend to, but these paled in importance to being there with my kids that night, or spending hours the next day helping Alex, Mikey's best friend since kindergarten, who was also in my class, write the eulogy for the service we all attended the next day.

Thankfully there is no call for that with Alyssa, who, though broken, will be back, will triumph over all that could not beat her. And so instead of eulogies, we wrote her notes today on the biggest get-well card I have ever seen. One of her friends brought it in for us after I asked her to get a card the class could sign. So it is that our work evolves, buffeted about like a sturdy but dented craft borne down the river of the year to the calm waters of summer when we can rest, reflect, and ready ourselves for the year that we will spend next week preparing for as the counselors come in to talk to the kids yet again about a future so many of them cannot imagine. But for now, I am glad to know Alyssa has and can prepare for that future once she gets out and gets back.

Jim

Jim:

The news is already spreading about this fifteen-year-old girl who committed suicide this week. My little sister, who is twelve years old, heard about it from a student in her class at middle school yesterday. She was informed by a friend, who I presume has an older sibling at a nearby high school, that the girl hung herself in her backyard. I can't imagine how this is stirring the students at the high school. It is unimaginable. Even more so, what if I had been her teacher? I suppose this is what this is really about. What if she were one of my students? How would I cope with such a horrific ending by choice?

I once had a student in Santa Cruz who always stunk of pot and finally shared later that her mother had committed suicide a few years back. She found nothing wrong with this and felt like it did not impact anyone else—it was her choice. I wholeheartedly disagree with her analysis. The choices we make, especially life-and-death ones, are going to shake anyone around us. It is my assumption that this girl has just not come to terms with what her mother did and the influence it has on her already tumultuous relationship with her father and others.

Once again the power of our role as teachers is strongly revealed. We are not simply teachers of reading and writing as you stated in your letter. There is so much more to it! We are not only imparting knowledge of a subject area but are also instructing our students about life. I think it is a potent thought I still remember my master teacher saying to me when I was frustrated with my first extremely difficult sophomore classes, that it is more important that the students learn from the characters in the books we read—like Hamlet and Lennie Smalls—what life is all about and how to navigate amidst its unpredictable waves. If they can learn from the mistakes of these characters, they will be better off.

Has a student of yours ever committed suicide? If so, what did you do? Or did you have students who openly told you they were suicidal? I was just wondering what you would do in this situation.

Joy

Dear Joy:

I remember it was sometime during my first year of teaching, and it was late on a weekend evening—too late to call anyone or do anything—when I read this boy's journal for my English class. In the journal, this kid, a very troubled boy, described in precise detail his preparations for slashing his wrists: the warm water running into the basin, the razor, the calm, the fear—and the sudden knocking on the door from his mother, who, without knowing it, saved her son's life. But I was too trapped in the effect of his detailed prose: I felt as though it were happening, as if I could stop what I soon realized had happened weeks earlier, for the student had been in class on Friday to turn in his journal. What remained with me was the feeling of helplessness coupled with a nagging sense that I should have seen it, should have noticed something. They spend fifty minutes a day with us, one of a herd of often angst-ridden teens, and yet we feel like we should know every detail of each student's life. But we cannot know them all so well, so we can only care and make sure they know that we care so if they do end up feeling the way that boy did, they can come to us. (By the way, to finish that story: I went to the counselors first thing Monday morning and had them summon the student . . .)

So it is that you ask one of the most troubling questions we face, yet which we so rarely face, though there are schools that suffer a string of suicides and homicides, each a consequence of the others, as if the first set them all free to fly away from all of this world's pain. To answer your question: Yes, I have had two students kill themselves and known of others, but a few others have forced their way into my classroom through my students' experience, most recently (and relevant to the girl in your letter) a Japanese American boy who hung himself a couple of years ago in eighth grade, an event that stained his classmates with a knowledge that surfaces in class during certain discussions, though no one likes to bring it up, as if his death were a source of shame to them all.

While I did not emphasize it in my last letter, it was clear to everyone who knew him and saw him with open eyes that Mikey's car accident was a suicide. There were no skid marks leading up to the concrete pillar. Witnesses spoke of him doing up to ninety miles an hour. And it was consistent with other patterns of behavior. The other student, however, was unexpected, though in retrospect not such a surprise. Cassandra was a freshman who didn't know who she was, where she belonged, or why she was here. She followed her friends because she didn't know where to lead herself. On occasion her friends would come to me (I was a first-year teacher) and say that Cassandra was talking about suicide. I knew only one thing from various trainings: you take every threat seriously. The logic, as I understand it (and Cassandra illustrates), is that if you ignore signs or dismiss their gestures, kids will become determined to prove to you how serious they are and thus will put themselves at greater risk.

And this is what Cassandra did: She grew tired of all her friends saying, "Oh, Cassandra, you're not going to kill yourself." And even when she did, she didn't mean to: she just wanted them to pay attention, to take her seriously—except by then it was too late. This fiery girl, not entirely unlike your student Amanda, who worked with kids at the preschool when my class went over to read to them, took a bunch of pills, intending to cause trouble, to get attention, except they caused effects she had not foreseen: her respiratory system failed and she died in the ER of complications.

My take on it is that such a kid gets trapped in a feeling of despair that suggests it will always be this way, *they* will always be this way. And so, lost in the forest of their own depression, unable to see the light, they destroy themselves, leaving in their wake a measure of pain that no one can ignore. I had a girl a few years ago who was so out of control; on looking further into it, I found out that her sister had killed herself and that the mother was *so* terrified that she would do the same thing that the mother did nothing, never intervened, never challenged her daughter—and all out of love, of a sort.

So what *do* you do if you are the teacher? First, you don't pretend to be able to do what you cannot: handle it on your own. You go to the counselors and ask for guidance. When a student dies, whether by suicide, accident, or murder, the school shuts down emotionally, becomes somber, stunned. I remember when Mikey died, big strong boys in my class, kids who had known him since childhood, would come in and say, "Mr. B., I gotta just go across the way [I had a separate room with a few computers in it across the hall] and write some poems. I can't stop thinking about Mikey." The counselors had kids write letters to him, saying to him whatever they needed to say: some screamed their anger; others expressed their sympathy, their love. During the days right after a death, especially by suicide, there is an aura of danger, as if others might follow that student's example. In a strange, modern twist on his death, the assistant principal had confiscated Mikey's cell phone the day before the accident; for days after he died, the phone would ring suddenly in Mr. Saroyan's office, keeping alive the feeling that he was still around somehow.

Most important is to watch over them, to sometimes protect them from themselves by letting them know you are watching, that they matter. It is unbelievable to me sometimes how kids can fall through the cracks, disappear into suicidal despair or chronic absence, which, when you learn more, you find means they've been sitting at home all day by themselves doing nothing and getting more depressed. I mentioned Jenny to you today when I saw you in class: She was in my class last year as a freshman. She missed approximately 85 percent of the school year, cutting, doing who knows what. When I saw that she was back this year, that she was getting a B– average at one point, I just could not believe it and had to go talk to her. And now this semester she is in your class and you probably would never guess that last year she was the student I have described.

We watch out for them because their parents can't (during the day) or don't know how, or don't care to try. I was reminded of the importance of watching out for kids just this week when a senior in my AP English class, a quiet Asian boy named Arnold, missed his ninth consecutive day. No note, no calls. I stopped his counselor and learned that he was unaware of Arnold's absences. The attendance office knew nothing. And so I asked friends, only to find that he had few at school. So I grew nervous. And then finally, only because I had initiated this inquiry, he returned, but only after meeting with the counselor to tell him that someone at school had threatened to kill him if he came back. So this poor boy, who is on the newspaper staff, who is in advanced classes, whose parents were away on business trips, and who should only be waiting for news of his college acceptance, was instead cowering at home, wondering what to do, afraid to tell anyone.

I am reasonably quick to inquire about the well-being of a kid if I have any concern. After the Columbine High School massacre, people said over and over that there were signs teachers and counselors should have read. I don't want to realize after it's too late that a student is in trouble, so I ask, I confront (gently), I watch, and if the student inspires enough concern, I go to the counselor and just say, "You know, I'm worried about this kid. Could you bring them in to just check in with them, see if they are doing OK?"

Schools can be such lonely, alienating places for kids, especially those who might be suffering depression or just feel isolated. It's one reason I say hi to kids all day. Kids notice it. And though it is cliché by now, I am always mindful of the story, perhaps taken from one of the Chicken Soup books, of the boy who grew so depressed that he planned his suicide but, thankfully, gave himself one more day to think about it. He decided that if he went through one more day of school without anyone saying anything to him, without so much as a hi, then he would cash it in. And the day had almost passed—he was at his locker, in the hall alone—when one of the star athletes walked by and just said, "Hey," and it was enough: he didn't go through with it. So you throw these lines out, even words as small as *hi*, and you hope they stick. Once a senior wrote me a note to say that when she was a freshman I had taken her into the hall and simply told her that she mattered. I had no memory of it. She said those few words made all the difference in the world to her and she never forgot them. But I did. Still, I say these things all the time in the hope that they will keep some student of mine from following Mikey or Cassandra into the next world before they have had time to learn to live and find all there is to love in this world.

I will close with a poem I was given years ago. It seems to have a whole new relevance in light of the emphasis on scores and testing in the current era:

SO HE DREW

He always wanted to explain things,
but no one cared,
So he drew.

Sometimes he would just draw and it wasn't anything.
He wanted to carve it in stone or write it in the sky.
He would lie out on the grass and look up in the sky
and it would be only the sky
and all the things inside him that needed saying.
And it was after that that he drew the picture,
It was a beautiful picture. He kept it under his pillow and would let
   no-one see it.
And he would look at it every night and think about it.
And when it was dark and his eyes were closed he could see it still.
And it was all of him and he loved it.
When he started school he brought it with him,
Not to show anyone, but just to have it with him like a friend.

It was funny about school.
He sat in a square brown desk like all the other square desks and he
   had thought it would be red.
And his room was a square brown room, like all the other rooms.
And it was tight and close. And stiff.
He hated to hold the pencil and chalk, with his arm stiff and his feet

flat on the floor, stiff, with the teacher watching and watching.
The teacher came and spoke to him.
She told him to wear a tie like all the other boys.
He said he didn't like them and she said it didn't matter.

After that they drew. And he drew all yellow and it was the way he
   felt
about morning. And it was beautiful.
The teacher came and smiled at him. "What's this?" she said.
"Why don't you draw something like Ken's drawing? Isn't it
   beautiful?"
After that his mother bought him a tie and he always drew airplanes
and rocket ships like everyone else.
And he threw the old picture away
And when he lay out alone looking at the sky, it was big and blue, and
   all of everything, but he wasn't anymore.

He was square and brown inside and his hands were stiff.
And he was like everyone else. All the things inside him that needed
saying didn't need it anymore. It had stopped pushing. It was crushed.
Stiff.
Like everything else.

(*Note:* This was written very quietly by a teenage boy in class. After-
ward he put it very quietly on his teacher's desk and went home and
quietly, very quietly, took his own life.)[1]

A heavy letter, a serious subject, but an important one to think about and
be prepared to address. Thanks for asking about it.

Your colleague,

Jim

Question 19

What is your relationship with parents?

⌐

Dear Joy:

Because you are a young, single teacher still living at home with yours, it is impossible for your to imagine being a parent. We think we can: after all, we *have* parents and have watched them for years, so what's not to know? Yet the truth is that you just cannot know until you are one. In a department of roughly fifteen teachers, you will count *only* three of us with young children living at home (I'm the only one whose kids are in school), and one of those children (Melissa's) is so new to the world that her cute little umbilical cord is still drying and preparing to fall off. Three others in the department have adult kids who have been gone from the house so long the parents have little sense of what it is to be a parent in this era. All the others have no children, which makes it all the more difficult for them to fathom why parents feel or act as they do. In fact, parents have become such a serious concern, such a paradox for teachers—we want them to be involved but only so far, to help but only so much, to push but only so hard, to visit but only so often—that *Time* magazine's latest issue carries this cover story: "What Teachers Hate About Parents."[1] My favorite part of the article is the categories into which teachers divide different types of parents:

- *Helicopter parents*: Those who are always hovering over the kids and the teachers and, ultimately, get in the way of the kids' ability to become self-reliant.
- *Monster parents*: "The lurking moms and dads always looking for reasons to disagree" and who are therefore "a teacher's worst nightmare."
- *Dry-cleaner parents*: People who drop their child off in the morning and want to pick them up at the end of the day all cleaned up and proper, ready to go.

I think the most honest, personal thing I can say *as a parent* of three kids (twelve, ten, and six; two boys and girl) is that it is a very anxious time to be a parent. Everyone wants things to work out for their kids, for them to be successful, happy, safe, and so on. As the world has become more competitive, it has become more difficult to trust that it will all just work out. You do everything you can, it's all working out, and then the car accident. You do everything you can to support your child's success in school and then (in San Francisco) they ignore your request for a neighborhood school and send your son across town to one of the most at-risk schools, leaving you to question whether you can support the public school system. You do everything you can, and your kids somehow find their way into the wrong crowd. Or, it simply works out, as it does for most people.

We live in a society that allows us to go into Starbucks and order a triple-shot, half-caf, extra-foam, 128-degree, latte with soy milk and cinnamon sprinkle but offers us little or no choice about some of the most fundamental aspects of our children's education: which classes they take, who their teacher is, which school (in some cases) they go to. We have become such a ravenous consumer society, expecting control over our experience and choice at every step of the way, only to find school the way it was when we went. I'm not sure I can say the center will hold for years to come. Some political theorist, commenting on China's political reforms, described his "pizza toppings theory of political revolution" this way: if everyone can have only cheese, then there is no trouble; as soon as people can decide between cheese and pepperoni, they think they should also get to choose their political leaders, since who runs the country is a much more important decision. Between the Internet, charter schools, private schools, and home-schoolers, it is hard to imagine schools will be able to afford to remain the way they are for the twenty years I have left in the profession.

Meanwhile, this *is* the world I work in, this is how the schools work, and the students I teach come with the parents they have. In my experience, parents are reasonable and supportive if they know you care and do your best. Teachers around school who complain the most about parents are, with a few exceptions, the kind of teachers who undermine our profession's reputation in the eyes of the public. I have taught for fifteen years and the number of problems I have had with parents is so small I can count them on one hand. And ultimately, as the letters included later show, if you are reasonable (and they are, too!), you can be real and honest and through that process help each other be better parents and teachers.

Which brings us to this last week, when I made a Big Mistake. I was taking my ACCESS class on a field trip to UC Berkeley for the day. We spent six months preparing for it, the point being to show them what a four-year university looks like so they would be inspired to work harder. And the Monroe twins both forgot to get the required signatures until the morning of the trip. Tyler was failing all his classes, mine included; what possible reason could he have to go? But his brother Tim was doing better, so I let him go. Rick Curwin, one of the few great professors I had in my credential program years ago, once said, "Teachers make ten thousand decisions a day and they all matter."[2] At the time this seemed silly, but a day like last Tuesday reminds you how true it is. I decided that this was the chance to wake Tyler up, to give him a reality check. I told him he could not go. I knew this was certain pain and a real blow, but that seemed all the more reason to do it. What I had not considered was the impact doing that would have on his twin. I might make the same decision again for the same reasons next time, but I'd get a bit further in front of it to avoid the trauma that ensued, though even that, ultimately, brought about important benefits for me, Tyler, and his mother.

So our class went off to have a great day at Berkeley, and we came home at the end of the day. I was about to go home happy about all I had done for my kids that day, when Rick Kell, the dean, asked me if I had heard about Tyler Monroe. I said I had not. The short of it is that he took off, everyone was looking for him, and eventually his mother found him at home, very upset.

I will let the letters that follow tell the story from there.[3]

Mr. Burke,

I left you a few voice mails today. I think you may have more than one voice mail . . . I heard two separate out going messages. I tried two ways of getting through to you, so you may have to check both if that is the case.

I would like to add that in your communication with Tyler today, you mentioned Suzanne choosing the wrong path. Again you obviously don't know what is happening with her. That's O.K. I don't expect you to know about her. However, I really wish you would educate yourself before you pass judgment or make severe decisions like you did with Tyler today. For the record Suzanne has been diagnosed with some really difficult emotional problems. She has learning disabilities and through all of this has always done her best. Unfortunately, she failed Algebra 2 twice and even with Resource help has not been able to pass Geo Stats. Because of this she would not be able to graduate next year if she remained at BHS. The decision to go to Penn was a tough one but one we decided was best for her. As far as you not wanting Tyler to end up there as well, none of us want that, yet it may be a reality. I am just amazed that you felt that you knew what was best, and felt the need to make that "statement" with your actions today. I know that you took it upon yourself to speak to the history teacher . . . all of Tyler's teachers signed that permission slip. You must have known before this morning that Tyler would not be going. I know that you feel strongly about treating the boys as individuals. That's not what you did today. You treated them differently but not in a fair and just way. I know a lot of the kids in your class, and I would imagine that some of them must have failing grades and that some of them would be a "distraction" as well. Maybe you weren't trying to make a statement with them. If you had really wanted to make a difference Mr. Burke, you could have gotten some input from his parents or Judy Werner the school psychologist even. Tim is smarter, he is far more assertive, he has self-esteem, He is a *great kid*. Tyler does not have those same strengths, he is a frustrated, depressed child. What's so sad is that this has only manifested this year. We have been trying to help him and believe me, what you have done is *not* helpful.

Joan

Dear Mrs. Monroe:

Thank you for your letter, and for all that you said. I do genuinely appreciate it. I will begin by saying simply that I am sorry I upset you; it was not my intention. I'm grateful for all the information you shared, and want to take time to address your different concerns and comments. I should say that I have not heard your phone messages as the phone in my room has not worked for some time and, as the service mentions, I find it easier to communicate by email. So forgive me if you raise questions in your voice mail message that I don't address here.

Let me begin with Suzanne, for this was the part of your email that troubled me the most. Communication with kids at school in classes takes place on the run, so we must try to do our best but very quickly. My strategy is to communicate using what is most familiar to the student so they can, in the instant, understand what I am saying. I only referred to the crisis one reaches when they cannot mathematically (because they lack units) graduate from BHS, and alluded to Suzanne's situation to illustrate. This was, as you say in your email, not appropriate (I agree with you in retrospect). You must understand, however, that I have in my mind only the highest regard for Suzanne, can tell you things she said in class as a freshman, work I held up in class as an example to others; so I have always seen only her potential to be successful and have always thought she was a wonderful girl. I accept responsibility for having used an insensitive example to make my point with Tyler, I must emphasize that I meant no disrespect to you or to Suzanne. As I said when speaking to her the other day as we three stood before the counseling office, Peninsula is, as you say, the best solution for her.

As for the field trip, there are a few points to clarify. The history teacher sought me out, told me that she was not going to sign for him to go; on top of that, I had told him the week before (when he returned from being out for so long) that he needed to stay in class and catch up in his classes. When I asked him why he wanted to go, he said "I don't know." The decision, though it does not look like it in the light of our current discussion, was based on my commitment to his success in school. Your email highlights the importance of effective communication (between school and home, teacher and student, parents and teachers, and parents and students) and I will work to do a better job from here on out. Indeed, your letter to me today will help me do a much better job. Sometimes parents communicate with me (or other teachers) what they are doing to, as you say, "try to help" their kids; in this way I have more context and can make better decisions. I would hope my error in this instance will not jeopardize your faith in me and my commitment to your two boys.

Thank you for writing, Mrs. Monroe, and for listening. I hope when I see you next we can see each other as allies and help each other help your boys be their best selves. There is no more important work.

Sincerely,
Jim Burke

Mr. Burke,

Thank you for your response. I do wish you had heard my voicemails. Please keep in mind that I was feeling very hurt and worried for and about my child. I don't mean to beat a dead horse, so to speak, but I really wish you would have handled this situation prior to the morning of the field trip. Raising identical twins is at times challenging, frustrating, nerve racking, wonderful and heartbreaking. All of these things are true for raising singletons as well, but I think you understand the unique challenges with twins. One of the frustrations is outside opinions on just how things should be handled, especially regarding their individualism. I can assure you that their father and I feel that as well. Of course they *are* individuals, but they are also extremely alike. Their own self-esteem and identity is (like it or not) almost completely wrapped up in the other's. They fight to pull out of that as much as they fight to stay in it. I feel strongly that they need to do this on their own. I have watched them grow and latch on to their own personalities and desires. They love each other and hate each other. They protect each other and torture each other. All in a much more intense and deeper fashion than normal siblings. This last year has been a complete change with these two. Between you and I, Tim has always been assertive and even kind of cocky. He however was the child in our family who was too risky, defiant, cocky to other adults, Tim used to be the kind of person who believed anything he did was just if he felt hurt. Tyler, Suzanne, Steve, myself and the general population have all felt his unreasonable (at times) wrath.

He has become reasonable, loving, cooperative, understanding of consequences and is showing more self-restraint. Ever since Tyler was an infant he was sweet, sensitive, consciencious, communicative, his teachers *loved* him. One BIS teacher used to call him the class caregiver. He has always been sort of overshadowed by his brother.

He has become a different person. He is angry and frustrated, he has no self-esteem and instead of feeling liked by his teachers, he feels dumb, confused and lost at school. He feels that it is futile to even try in his classes. He blames himself but that just perpetuates the problem even more. I think his depression has started to affect his perception.

When outside forces force separation in an unnatural or unfair way it only makes this independence and sense of self more difficult for them to find.

I'm sorry to go on and on, I would just like to assure you that we consider them individuals and treat them as such. Their consequences and rewards are based on behavior. When they both deserve a reward they both get one. If they both deserve a punishment, they both get one. However, they are not treated as a unit unless they act like one.

I would also like to assure you that I have the utmost regard for you as a teacher and a mentor. I know that you genuinely care about these kids. your intentions are wonderful. I am very disappointed in your actions, but I do trust your intentions, I only wonder if your motivation was based on the twin issue rather than a Tyler issue. If it was then I hope this has helped you to have a better understanding.

I will of course continue to consider you an ally. I hope you will continue to feel the same (even after you hear the voice mails).

Even though this situation was less than desirable, I want to thank you for your commitment to my children and all of these kids whose lives you touch. If every teacher had the caring and commitment that you show . . . well let's just say how wonderful that would be.

Sincerely,

Joan

Dear Mrs. Monroe:

I'm so glad you wrote back this evening as our exchange has been on my mind all day. I listen to all you say with the ears of a teacher and a parent and I hear it clearly. All your thoughts about the kids and twins are immensely helpful and give me useful insights. I have to say, the nature of schools these days is becoming increasingly difficult for a boy like Tyler. There seems to be less and less room for the compassion we want to see from teachers and schools who feel immense pressure to meet the highest standards of academic performance. For the kids who are ready to jump higher and farther, the climate of acceleration and increased expectations is a tonic to the system, a good thing. But for a kid like Tyler who feels as you describe, he needs sanctuary and support, something I will have to work hard to convince him I can still provide, but which you must also help him find in the year ahead until he gets his footing.

I also found your comments about the dynamic between them very interesting and useful, particularly in light of something I saw today in class. Tim, as you mention in this last email, can be pretty hard on Tyler, taking advantage of opportunities to put him down in ways that catch me off guard every time (and which I try to talk to him about as quickly as possible). Today, when the kids were finished with their silent reading, Tyler was casting about for a pencil to do the assignment with, and Tim saw this and tossed him (from two rows over and four seats back) a pencil and said in a very supportive, encouraging voice, "Here you go, Ty. Keep it so you don't have to ask in other classes later on." This was in stark contrast to how he has talked to him in the past and I was quite moved by it. And when we went around the room to solicit the words kids had written down, Tyler was all set, had a good word to offer up, and was a good member of the team.

I'm grateful for your expression of faith and commitment to continuing to work together in the future. I don't know if you'll get this in time to respond back with a suggestion, but in the morning I will work with the class on a thank you letter to Berkeley. I am going to ask Tyler to write to me and share his thoughts with me about this event and I will use that occasion to write him back a very encouraging letter. I also need to meet with him to prepare for his second speech on Friday for Toastmasters. You might check in with him about that as he needs to come Friday prepared to give a two minute speech on a subject of his own choosing. I might suggest that he give a talk about how high school is different from middle school, or to discuss some rule that he tries to follow in life. I try to get them to reach for a bigger idea for their second speech. Ultimately, however, he should choose a topic he can get up and speak about with confidence so he can be successful.

Please don't hesitate to write me any time if you think there is something I can do to help or something I should know about, Mrs. Monroe. I want to thank you again for your faith in me: It's something I've come to appreciate more and more as I send my own two sons, and this year my kindergarten-aged daughter, out into the world and the hands of others on whom I must rely.

Sincerely,
Jim Burke

Hi Mr. Burke,

Thanks for your support, it means a lot to us. I think that your idea sounds good. Please keep in mind that Tyler may not be very forthright with what he has to say in his letter. But who knows, he surprises me sometimes. I am so glad that I was able to read your letter before bed. I am so grateful for your help, and hearing about Tim being kind to his brother was a nice note to end the day. Those acts of kindness between them are too few these days. Tim has a way of creating moments at home that make him feel good about himself and know that we approve of and support him. With Tyler I have to be more creative, try to draw him out and find out how to help.

I didn't know that you had three children! I should have known, you can tell by how much thought you put into your job. Although I am a bit surprised that you have the energy!

Joan

Mrs. Monroe:

Today was very different than I expected: I forgot we had a guest speaker coming in. You should ask the boys about it: they both asked four questions each (I keep track of participation) and good questions. I was short some copies of something and asked Tyler if he could go handle this business for me, and made a point at the end of the period of shaking his hand a good one and apologizing. The boys (as with all the others) were really into the speaker who was a great guy (an FBI Special Agent!).

If you could follow-up with Tyler on his speech tomorrow that would be so helpful. He goes first and it is two minutes long. I gave him a sheet today that should help him prepare his ideas. Thanks for helping Tyler out if you can tonight. He can call me at home if he feels stuck. I will be out for a bit to go to my son's middle school concert but should be back by 8ish.

Jim Burke

Mr. Burke,

I was working until quite late last night, but I did rouse Tyler. He said he had worked on the speech. This morning I had him show me. . . . It wasn't very long and I was a bit concerned. He said that he practiced it with his father. I am keeping my fingers crossed.

He did seem upbeat about his relationship with you. I told him how impressed I was with you, and explained that even though we may not have agreed on this situation (at the time) I believe that you completely had his best interests in mind. He agreed.

I rarely give in to such emotion, at least outwardly, as I did the other day. Most of what I had to say was coming straight from my feelings and were totally relevant if not frantic. But those comments were just out of anger and completely inappropriate. I unfortunately did not follow my Sleep on It rule.

Again you have my sincerest apology.

Joan

Could I interact this way with the hundred-plus parents I have this year, some of whom live happily together in the same house, others of whom are gone on business trips and sometimes ask for personal emails daily (which I don't provide), still others of whom are split up, their kids alternating between the two homes, and so on? Of course not. But this was the right situation in which to follow through in this way. I also made six calls home this week to different parents for different reasons and asked the counselors to follow up with other parents on issues more appropriate to their area of expertise.

At the risk of dragging this already too-long letter out, I want to include a different exchange with a mother, in this case a very involved mother of a kid I enjoy teaching very much and who was recently accepted into Harvard. I'll let the exchange speak for itself:

Mr. Burke:

I have been reading Alexander's papers and appreciate your comments (even if it is "C" work with "I know what I can expect from you Mr. Park, and won't accept less than your best"). They are very informative and encouraging. Like you, I know Alexander is capable of "A" work, and I am glad you are there to push him. My constant concern is that my kids have been able to pull "A's" in English, without really deserving them. It may be good for their egos (while in high school), but it hurts them in college.

I hope you'll keep the bar high (even at the risk of Alexander not graduating as valedictorian of his class—though I hope it will not come to that).

Thanks,
Evelyn Park

Dear Mrs. Park:

Thanks so much for the kind note. You've mentioned on several occasions the idea that Alex might not be valedictorian as a result of my class. As you are well aware, we are all responsible for our own success. Please encourage him to do the work he must at the level he must to achieve such honors. Repeatedly mentioning it in correspondence—he has done the same—might give the unintended impression of exerting pressure to ensure an outcome. I *will* keep the bar high, and know Alex will work hard to clear it and earn the honors he seeks.

Sincerely,
Mr. Burke

Mr. Burke:

First, I'd like to clear any possible misunderstanding regarding how I conduct/conducted myself—my style is to speak what's on my mind, instead of hinting or "pressuring to ensure an outcome." Having raised 3 children, I find a clear message to be much more effective—no wasted time nor room for misunderstanding. Hence, if I am appreciative, I will say so, and if I'm disgruntled, I am equally direct.

Second, I am puzzled at the comment of "repeatedly mentioning it in correspondence"—to the best of my knowledge, I have contacted you twice (since school started, not including the recent email on 1/21). The first time was an email on 10/5 (around the first progress report period) and then a note before Christmas with a small gift (a customary gesture to all my children's teachers, since nursery school). Perhaps I mentioned (?) the valedictorian issue in the Christmas note (which I do not recall, as I do not have a copy of it), for I sure did not address it in my 10/5 email. In fact, this is what I wrote in the email dated 10/5 after learning that Alexander was not doing well in English. . . . "Thank you *very* much for being tough on Alexander and holding the bar high, I support you 110 percent! Most everything comes so easily to Alexander, except writing which is his relative weakness. If you hold him to a *really high* standard now, eventually he will realize the gift you have given him. He's gotten so used to minimum input maximum output, that he does not always apply himself. Please keep pushing him. You are right(!) he is capable of good work—I gather his latest homework proved it. He felt proud about the 'A' he received on the last homework, he felt he *earned* it! I hope you will keep him on his toes for the rest of the year."

Third, I mentioned the valedictorian issue in my recent email, because I know Alexander emailed you about it. I wanted you to know that I *support* your high standards—even if it means Alexander will not be class valedictorian (this is not to imply you need my support, and there were no other hidden messages at all!).

Fourth, I am in absolute agreement with you, that students should earn their grade/honor, otherwise (to me) the honor/grade is hollow and somewhat meaningless. Worse yet, it gives the student a false sense of one's ability/preparedness, and this is misleading/disastrous when one wishes to enter a top-notch university and compete with the best. Having witnessed Caroline, our eldest's acclimation to Harvard in '95, I quickly learned that a very rigorous high school curriculum is essential preparation for an Ivy League college. All her friends (from public high schools) have echoed her sentiment, that even though they/she took on the toughest academic load, it was still not preparation enough. This was especially evident when it came to writing, for despite being a hard working and talented writer (a gift recognized even by her Harvard teacher), Caroline had to struggle to make the huge adjustment to Harvard's standards. The transition from a public high school into an Ivy League college is very tough, so I am thankful for all the help that teachers offer, when they hold the bar high.

Last, I will absolutely admit that when the first progress report came home, I felt sad that Alexander might miss being class valedictorian. For surely he has taken on the toughest academic load available (in or out of BHS), a load so rigorous few students (if any) have taken on, so if anyone has earned that honor, he should have . . . were it not for his English grade. Despite that concern, I also felt *strongly* that if he didn't work hard at English, he did *not* deserve to graduate as class valedictorian—a sad consequence but a reality in life! In our discussion about the valedictorian issue, Alexander took responsibility for his poor English grades (a lack of sufficient effort on his part, versus lack of ability). He understood that unless he puts in the needed effort for his English, he would not graduate with the honor. But more importantly, I was comforted to know that he decided to give his best effort in English, because he recognized the importance of improving his writing skills, and class valedictorian standing was a secondary concern. At this point, his focus is on becoming a better writer, a goal he enjoys pursuing, and whatever happens will happen, and he's fine with it (and so am I).

Sorry the email is so long, but I wanted you to understand where I am coming from, and to clear the air. . . .

Thanks,
Evelyn Park

Thanks for taking the time to write, Mrs. Park. I meant no offense and appreciate the commitment you have to your three kids and their education. I also appreciate honest communication; the world needs more of it. I'll just end by saying that I've had talks with Alex this year that have been among my favorite moments as I learn how to live with and teach seniors. My oldest is 12 and I would be awfully proud if he grew up to be the kind of young man Alex is. Looking forward to the rest of the year.

Sincerely,
Jim Burke

Mr. Burke,

I wasn't (terribly) offended, I just wanted to set the record straight, so that there is no room for misunderstanding.

Thank you for your touching compliment about Alexander. I believe the admiration is mutual. He's mentioned the wonderful conversations he's had with you—discussions about life in general as well as classroom "stuff." Thank you from the bottom of my heart for your mentoring and guidance.

A little background about my "fixation" on writing (a skill the kids will need for the rest of their lives)—during Caroline's junior parent weekend at Harvard, I read an article in the Harvard newspaper, on how the university was (and still is) trying to focus effort on improving their students' writing skills, because they felt the students were not prepared enough (and these are the cream of the crop we are talking about!). They identified in particular, the need to teach "subject specific writing"—they recognized that the skills needed to write a good paper are different from subject to subject (e.g., philosophy versus English). Given Caroline's transition to Harvard and the info from that article, I started to focus on building a good writing foundation for Matthew and Alexander. Despite writing workshops and summer courses in Expository writing, I still feel their writing is not solid enough.

In the same paper, I also read a "horror" story about how a past editor of the *Crimson* (Harvard's newspaper) was reduced to tears when she was in a freshman writing class. How, despite obvious talent in writing, she doubted her ability in the early years there. Both Caroline and Matthew can vouch for the rigorous writing standards they've been subjected to!

Harvard students expressed the need for feedback—this was something they desired the most, in order to improve their writing. I understand grading an English paper is much more time consuming than say a math paper or a multiple choice paper, which is why when you spend time to make comments, know that it is highly valued (good or bad). I can't speak for others, but I know in Alexander's case, your high standards, your time and effort are greatly appreciated.

Thanks for making a mark in Alexander's high school life! I too, look forward to a wonderful rest of the year!

Evelyn

P.S.: Alexander was planning on kicking back, shifting into "cruise" so that he can enjoy the rest of his senior year . . . thank goodness you're there to make him work :-)

Mrs. Park:

A couple things you might find interesting. First, I happened to pick up a copy of the *Harvard Business Review* this weekend (while traveling to Texas) and it included an incredible article by Peter Drucker called "Managing Oneself."[4] I immediately planned to copy it for Alex, though I haven't had time (I got home late last night). Second, one of the more interesting books I have read while researching my last two books is *Making the Most of College*, by Richard Light; it is actually about the Harvard student orientation program.[5] The first thing they found with *all* successful kids is that they established a meaningful, sustained connection to at least one adult mentor. The second thing that successful students had in common was the role writing played in their success and developing an identity of themselves (by becoming good writers) as able to play in the big leagues. It's a book you would find interesting and no doubt would explain your older kids' success.

Regards,
Jim Burke

Mr. Burke:

Thank you for your article and book suggestion, I will certainly look into it.

I don't want to leave you with the impression that Alexander may not be ready for Harvard, for he surely is (besides, "ready" is all relative). If anything, Alexander is probably the *most* prepared of the 3 kids. Getting first hand input from Caroline and Matthew helps tremendously, both for preparing Alexander's transition to college and for helping me become a better parent (a never ending process . . .).

I welcome any advice you may have to offer, so please feel free to share with me what you feel is appropriate.

With appreciation and thanks,
Evelyn

This letter exchange paints a complex picture about the relationship between teachers and parents, Joy. In these letters I tried to take a professional stance that was both sympathetic and authoritative, a difficult balance but one we must try to strike if we are to be seen as a professional and not a store clerk they can push around till they get what they want. In one other situation this year the problem was so unreasonable I referred it to the administration because clearly the mother was going to make me her special project. Her son, who is in my AP class, cut thirty classes in the fall, spending most of them (as she herself emailed to tell me, so I "wouldn't worry") sleeping in his car in the parking lot because his depression was preventing him from doing the work in my class. When he took the final exam and received a B+ on it, this was confirmation (to her) of the genius she thinks he is, so she demanded that I give him a B+ in the class instead of the D– he had rightfully (and just *barely*) earned. After a series of emails that did not result in me completing her order, she went to the administration, which has since (again, after *weeks* and *many* emails) helped her understand how the world (of school, at least) works. By letting the administration handle that, I was free to continue on with the business I am paid to do: teach!

I'll end with this: When I began these letters to you, I wrote with the intention of helping you succeed and better understand your work and how to do it; it has become clear to me, as the year has unfolded and we've continued this conversation, that the letters are as much to myself, for in this climate of change, this era when our work and our personal and professional integrity are so routinely questioned by parents, politicians, and the public at large, I need to know what I stand for, why I do this work. I can only hope these letters do that half as well for you as they have for me this year.

Sincerely,

Jim

Interlude 6

JUGGLING THE DEMANDS
OF TEACHING AND LIVING

❧

Wow. What a letter! So much to think about. I find it difficult to balance my desire to be a "hero" to my students, the teacher who will help them succeed and do all they need to do to become great, and the overwhelmed twenty-one-year-old in me thinking "What am I doing here? I am not capable of being/doing all this! I can still pass for a student at times!" Amidst all this is the turmoil I feel constantly at my tardiness in returning their papers back to them and the limited comments I give them because I never feel like I have enough time to do anything—school for them and school at SJSU. In addition, physically my body is not twenty-one. My constant dull ache in my back, which is heightened at times, has now spread to my hips, making it difficult to walk without feeling the pain. I don't show it, or at least try not to, but this is yet another thing weighing on me. I have the passion to be a great teacher and feel so wanting of the tools. But, I am trying to remember that I simply must give it my best and leave the rest up to God.

Thanks for letting me vent. Your letters are indeed helpful in guiding/developing my own pursuit of who I am as a teacher.

Joy

Dear Joy:

I'll begin by answering with an image.

It's 7 P.M. after a long day of work and all the big people (parents) are sitting uncomfortably in the bright red fifth-grade chairs in Ms. Cheung's fourth/fifth-grade class at Alamo Elementary School. Some of us know each other—those who have had kids pass through already. We chat idly, waiting for the bell to ring and the principal to call the school to order for Open House. The walls of the class are positively alive with student work, so much so that it seems almost aggressive in its desire to show how much work the kids are doing and how hard they are working! Ms. Cheung, a young teacher, has begun to blush before she even starts talking, but I'm thinking she should feel at ease because we all look so absurd folded into the little chairs. To entertain myself I peer into my son Whitman's desk, only to be assaulted by the chaos of it all. It looks like every paper he ever touched in elementary school is stuffed into the salad of his desk! But I have to pay attention now because she is beginning her pitch, her *spiel*. She talks too fast, perhaps afraid that someone will throw her a curveball. I think: "It's so nice to watch someone else in front for a change." The time passes in pleasant chat that allows us all to leave feeling like our children are loved, the teacher is committed, and she is doing her best to help the kids and herself improve. What more can we ask?

High school is not so different, but there a few things worth mentioning. First, there is Back to School Night (September) and Open House (March/April). BTSN is all about establishing your own credibility in the parents' eyes, assuring them you mean business and will deliver the goods; they come in wanting to know you have a game plan and the ability to carry it out. Because school is just beginning, BTSN tends to be pretty calm. If a teacher has had problems or the year has been a mess, Open House can be a bit more difficult because the year is nearing its end and the jury is coming to your room. I can tell you that you won't have anything to worry about because kids are so obviously happy to be in your class. Parents want their kids to learn and do well, but they also want them to be happy, to feel good about school since they cannot be with their kids during that part of the day.

At BTSN I usually put out the books and my syllabus; sometimes I will make available a sample assignment to show parents what we have been doing or are about to do. In September I am still getting to know the kids, so I pass out index cards and ask the parents to tell me things about their children I might not know, especially things that will help me teach them better. One year, for example, I had a mother write, "James has a severely disabled twin sister who is mentally retarded. He loves her but also has very confused feelings about things since she demands so much more time. He wouldn't want you to know I told you about this." That turned out to be very useful information. Other parents will tell you that they are recently divorced or that a favorite grandparent recently passed away. By Open House, however, the fix is in: the story of the year is mostly told and has little time for revision.

It's harder to dress up the room in high school the way the elementary school teachers do. You and I, for example, share a room with other teachers, so who owns the walls? And there are different subjects taught in the room, so it makes no sense to dress up the walls. Open House—at least this is how it has been in the past—follows no schedule like BTSN does; this means that parents from any kid in any of your periods can wander in. So I might have a struggling freshman's mother wanting to talk to me at the same time that a senior AP student's mom wants to know what I am going to do in the homestretch to help her son arrive at Harvard in the fall ready to go. Standing next to those two might be a former student's parents, who are stopping by to say hi and thanks, and perhaps to introduce me to their eighth grader, who is coming in the fall and whom they hope will be in my class. And behind them all might well be, especially at our school, a few stray parents of kids in seventh, fifth, even second grade(!) who are shopping the schools, thinking ahead, trying to decide whether they need to abandon the public schools and apply to private schools.

In short, Open House is a big PR night, and teachers are expected to look professional and be "on message" about the school, the curriculum, and each parent's son or daughter. It is *not* the venue for sudden parent conferences; if you have anyone who wants to talk to you about grades, say, "I'd be happy to talk to you about that, but that's not what tonight is for. Could we arrange to meet or talk later this week?" Don't even have your gradebook within a mile of the class that night. What you can do is write an open letter to parents that would fit for all classes—something akin to the often-mocked "Christmas letter"—and run off enough to pass out. Sometimes parents have as many as three kids they are running around campus to check on, and such a letter allows them to get more info than they have time or patience to gather. On it you can include your email address and anything you think will help the parents help their children.

Though a few years old, here is one such letter I just found:

Dear Parent(s):

Back to School Night often focuses on what teachers do to help students do better. This, of course, is appropriate and important; but I thought I would take a few minutes to suggest some ways you, too, can help your child succeed in school. The following list is not in any particular order, but all of the suggestions will help in one way or another.

- *Ask questions about what they are doing, what they are studying.* Of course grades matter, but if we reduce children's education down to "What grade are you getting in English?" kids will think they are only worth the grades they get.

- *Talk to your children about ideas.* The teenage years can be complicated as kids seek, sometimes awkwardly and without much grace, to be independent. While it can be difficult to talk to them about them, talking about the ideas they study or the issues in the news offers safe, valuable ground for substantial conversations.

- *Help them (learn to) take care of themselves.* Students today often work longer, harder hours than they used to; this is often due to the extracurricular activities and jobs they have in addition to schoolwork. To help them stay well: Eat healthy food. Not only do bodies not grow well on junk food, but minds do not work well on such useless fuel. Keep fruit and other healthy snacks around.

- *Get at least eight hours.* Most teens are sleep deprived. Some stay up late chatting online; others take longer to do their homework. Kids need sleep to grow, think, and work well.

- *Carry less weight.* Backpacks sag with up to 25 pounds of books, leaving many kids to resemble alpine adventurers. Help your child assess what they must carry, and what they can keep at home. In extreme cases, ask the school to provide an extra book so your child doesn't have to carry so much.

- *Set limits.* Between the telephone, television, and the Internet, kids can get *so* distracted, and lose lots of time. In this world of distractions, kids (and adults!) need to learn how to manage their attention. If they do not, they will work longer and yet learn less.

- *Help them become strategic learners.* Effective students have techniques they use to succeed and work efficiently. Work with your child to develop tricks and strategies that will teach them how to: (1) manage time; (2) set goals and priorities; (3) solve problems (social, emotional, academic); (4) work efficiently.

- *Help them do their work well—but on their own.* You never help your student if you do their work for them. If you help them with their writing, help them develop techniques to get started, revise, or otherwise improve their papers.

- *Provide what they need to do their work well.* This includes: (1) a computer; (2) a good, collegiate dictionary (e.g., *American Heritage Collegiate*, fourth edition); (3) supplies; (4) a quiet, dedicated place in which to work.

- *Ask their teachers what you can do.* Call or email your child's teacher; keep the lines of communication open. Ask not only how your child is doing but what you can do to help. Tell teachers what helps your child succeed. If there are events going on in the child's life that might affect their performance or behavior in school, let teachers know. We are in this together and must work together to help your child be the success we know they can be.

Please feel free to contact me via email via the school's website. If you don't know about schoolloop.com yet, please check that out, as that is an important way to stay informed about the work in all of your child's classes. Finally, thank you for taking the time to come tonight.

Sincerely,
Jim Burke

I like Open House very much. It's a celebration of not just the kids' work but *mine*. Not everyone comes, but those who do almost invariably are grateful (and take the time to tell you so) for your investment in their child's growth. While it's not appropriate to talk politics on such an occasion, you might find that they would appreciate some info on and insight into the exit exam, since you teach sophomores. Some of them (this year) might have questions about the new SAT, which you can answer, or if you aren't sure what to say, you can direct them to the counselors for answers. And since we're in the midst of enrolling kids for next year, you might have a few parents who'll want to discuss their child's placement next year. This is a different conversation than grades, so if you are comfortable talking about it and there are not people waiting, it is fine to talk to them about this issue since it is a pressing matter and you have important insights to offer.

So hook up with some teachers you enjoy, go out for a nice dinner of laughter and good food before, and come to the class confident you have brought the kids along this far and can complete the journey in the remaining few months. There is so little time left! So much still to do! Our work is simply never done, so as my master teacher Pat Hanlon said years ago, we do our best with the constant knowledge that we could do it better under more ideal circumstances.

Enjoy the weekend and be sure to plan ahead for Spring Break so you have something to look forward to that will prevent you from only working.

Your colleague,

Jim

Interlude 7
APPLYING FOR A NEW TEACHING JOB

⤳

To Whom It May Concern:

I have had the honor of watching Joy Krajicek teach English to her thirty-five sophomores all year long. I asked her if I could write this letter of recommendation and offer my observations as to why you should consider her and why she will become a remarkable teacher.

There is so much to learn when one becomes a teacher; it nearly overwhelms us all. Joy had the rare opportunity to begin her career this year with three classes, thus giving her time to prepare more carefully and reflect at greater length than most new teachers can. She took full advantage of this opportunity in ways that reveal the kind of person and teacher she is. Instead of "just teaching," she enrolled in graduate classes to improve her knowledge of academic writing, rhetoric, and literary theory at San Jose State. Instead of coming in silently to a room she had to share with an experienced colleague, she introduced herself and asked me to share with her whatever I thought might help her do her job better.

This small gesture, connecting with an experienced colleague, helps to explain why Joy has had a successful first year of teaching and will continue to grow and blossom as a teacher. The inherent isolation of teaching undermines so many would-be great teachers who encounter problems they do not yet know how to face. Joy, on the other hand, initiated a conversation that has continued throughout the year. I told her that she could ask me questions about anything that would help her be more effective and succeed. The next day she showed up with the first card, and the question was: How do you get reluctant students to do their work? This essential question signaled her commitment to all of her students, and everything I have witnessed in the ensuing months has only confirmed her faith in and commitment to all her students.

The sophomore English class is a crucial and difficult course for these students, for it is here that they must take the state exit exam; moreover, our district initiated a common assessment designed to find out where students stood so they could be better prepared for the upcoming state tests. Joy therefore had to learn all about the state standards and current state tests, something not all new teachers come to their jobs prepared to address.

All of my remarks here should be considered within the larger framework of my own work and reputation within the field: I am the author of twelve books about the teaching of English, several of which are used as core texts in teacher preparation and methods classes around the country. I helped revise the National Board for Professional Teaching Standards for Adolescents and Young Adults. Thus I could not afford to say the things I have said here if they were not true. Joy has much to learn; so do we all, especially in those first years. But she has demonstrated at every turn the commitment and ability to learn what she needs to be successful.

You can measure a teacher's effectiveness by many means these days, some of which are more valid than others. The most observable, however, has to do with the climate of a teacher's class. Do kids slink in there with the same joy they have when they go to the dean's office? Or do they greet the teacher by name and show evident pride that they did their work and have their materials? Do they sit silently, asking for help they believe the teacher will not offer? Or do they feel secure in the classroom and able to admit they do not know something or need help to do it better? Is it a classroom in which only the best and brightest are expected to succeed? Or is it a classroom where every student feels valued and is expected to do well, and is supported as needed to do their best?

The record of my year with Joy Krajicek is detailed in the 250 pages of letters I have written to her in response to her essential questions about the work of English teachers. She is neither my student teacher nor my BTSA-appointed teacher; rather she is my colleague and friend. Our conversations this year about teaching and students have taught me much. It is thus with great pride that I recommend her to you without reservation to teach English.

Sincerely,
Jim Burke
English Department
Burlingame High School

AVOIDING TROUBLE IN THE HOMESTRETCH AS TESTING SEASON BEGINS

Joy:

So . . . how did the job fair go?

A perfect day outside to spend in the office working on school stuff with Willie Nelson on in the background. . . . See you tomorrow.

Jim

~~~~~~

Jim:

The job fair went well. I saw two teachers I had in high school and quickly had an interview. It was a preliminary interview to be placed in their eligibility pool. The interview went well, but I had difficulty with it only being fifteen minutes. I felt sooooo rushed! I'll find out if I made it soon. Otherwise the process is long and tedious. . . . Who knows what will happen. :)

See you tomorrow.

Joy

~~~~~~

Hey Jim:

Just a heads-up that I might not be there tomorrow. I am stressing about some work I have to do for SJSU and I need to finish some grading (and possibly try and squeeze in a dr. appt. for my hip pain . . .). I feel like I have missed so much, but I am not sure if I can get everything finished. Any comments? Suggestions? I am really torn here between my different responsibilities and what I should do. What do you think?

Joy

~~~~~~

Joy:

I don't know all the factors, but here is something: They come back from break and need a strong hand to get them back in the saddle. Next week will already upset the apple cart with state testing all week, but if they come back and find you're gone that first day it could undermine the whole week and thus the next two. That said, if it's what you have to do (i.e., take the day), then plan like gangbusters for Tuesday and come in like the leader you need to be, thinking ahead about next week and what you can do with them under such circumstances. Are you even going to be able to be around next week with that crazy testing schedule? It's different (I believe) at each school, so it's likely to play havoc with your split realities of BHS and Mills. Ah, just when you thought things were getting easier . . . !

I'm just sitting here grading papers and planning. Call if you need to talk about any of this to figure it out. Really.

Jim

~~~~~~

Jim:

I have been mulling over what you've said for the past fifteen minutes. For my students' sake I will be there tomorrow and just suck it up and do the best I can with all that is on my plate. I don't want more chaos to weigh me down with how challenging my fourth period can be.

I will see you tomorrow. Thanks for the comments and thanks for your willingness to let me call you. It means a lot. Have a good night.

Joy

~~~~~~

Jim:

One other thought: do we have that special schedule on Wednesday (for meetings)? If I won't be there on Wednesday, then I don't want to miss tomorrow. It would be too crazy for my students.

Joy

~~~~~~

Oooh, good question, Joy! I think we do have one of those long mornings that will mess things up for you. If society had *any* idea how chaotic the school world can be—as a business it would not last a year!—they would marvel at us instead of yelling at us.

With this all in mind, it is important for you to sit down and plan not just for this week but the next three with the state tests in mind. What will you be able to accomplish? Don't say—as some do—*nothing*! Instead, think of the crazy sched-ule the way a poet might consider the limitations and constraints of the haiku or some other form; as the poet Richard Wilbur said of poetic form, "The strength of the genie derives from being kept in the bottle." So see the limits of the schedule this and next week as discrete spaces within which to work. Also, in case that was too easy, consider what kind of work will offer the chance for meaning and engagement but also create the opportunity to teach things that will help them on the state tests next week. I would consider working with some short poems and doing close reading and writing, and making some connections to test-taking (e.g., have them create sample test questions about the poems) that you can use for discussion questions, also. Hope this helps.

What might this look like? When I taught sophomores last time I brought in a poem by Yusef Komunyakaa called "Happiness" in his collection *Magic City.* The poem is a list of images of happiness from his childhood all blurred into an imag-istic poem. I had kids (sophomores) begin first solo and then huddle up to create a list of images of happiness, focusing on language and images; then we read and annotated Komunyakaa's poem and talked about what he was trying to accomplish in it and how he used these images, this language to accomplish that.

It seems like you might appreciate this poem ("If") by Kipling, one everyone knows, but one that is no less true for our knowing it.[1] It seems appropriate as you attempt to "keep your head" while all the world around you spins with demands and makes you feel like I did on the merry-go-round with my daughter last weekend at the amusement park.

See you in the morning.

Jim

Dear Joy:

Though it seems like there is a lot of time left, there is not: twenty days of actual class if you count the four days of state testing and the three days for final exams as lost; there are even fewer if you add in the assemblies and the time spent wrapping things up (collecting books, assembling portfolios, returning projects, giving culminating presentations, and so on). I don't say all this to scare you or hurl you into a state of panic, but rather to remind you that the year is moving along. This is what time does best: pass. And yet we all have certain needs that must be met if this remaining time is to satisfy students and teacher alike. In short, we must find a way to bring the year in for a decent landing so that as everyone steps down onto the tarmac of the summer months, they can look back and feel they traveled some distance from where they began and see us as having helped to get them there.

I can't help but recall those lines from T. S. Eliot's poem "Little Giddings":

What we call the beginning is often the end
And to make an end is to make a beginning.
The end is where we start from. And every phrase
And sentence that is right . . .
Every phrase and every sentence is an end and a beginning. . . .

We shall not cease from exploration
And the end of all our exploring
Will be to arrive where we started
And know that place for the first time.[1]

What brings this poem to mind? As I watch my seniors head toward graduation—every day seems to have some small step toward the rite of passage: today they were given a card on which to write out their name as they wish it to appear on their diploma—I am suddenly struck by the realization that this is not an ending but just the beginning of the life they must go out and create for themselves. I'm only forty-three, but my graduation was *twenty-five years ago*. To me, it is everything after that event that matters most. As for you, Joy, you are ending your first year but only beginning your career, your adult life. This year is merely "where [you] start from," and every day and year from here on out will be as some phrase or sentence in the longer, greater story of your professional life. And though you can think only of ending the year, hidden within that truth—that it *will* end—is the invitation to already begin dreaming the new year, the year when you will do it all better, guided by all you know from this year.

Still, I know this last stretch has been difficult. I know that because it has been difficult for *me*. While I do my best to soldier on in the midst of all the sound and fury going on around school lately, the truth is that I struggle myself in ways that are worth sharing. Though it has not touched you— because you are not full-time yet—many teachers have been going through a real firestorm as the district and school board have moved to impose cuts to save money. These troubles weigh on us all. Who could not feel some measure of compassion and grief when they read such an email as this one, sent to a colleague by a new teacher:

> I've been okay during all the talk about lay offs the past month or so. However, just yesterday, at end of the day, after my 3 hour class, I got to my door step and found the note from the post office to go pick up my pink slip . . . well I was down. I haven't felt this down in a looong time. I'm ok today, and I still believe as always that in the end, the very end . . . things always work out for the best. Honestly, though, I have a bit of doubt at where or what I want to be or do . . . as much as I love my kids, it makes me wonder how a district screws over 600 employees and expects us to pour our heart and souls into our jobs after they toss us around and toy with our minds like pawns. I just need some time to let this all sink in and go from there. I'm sorry. I'm frustrated. I know I can work elsewhere, but this is where I want to be. My students and I have poured our sweat, tears, energy together to build a community that has trust . . . they work hard for me and I for them. Now that's that. I'm a bit confused . . . love, Liz

I can't help seeing myself in my second year of teaching—the only time I have ever cried in front of students—as I sat in the front of the class holding my own pink slip (only about a month after being nominated by the principal for County Teacher of the Year!). All I could think of was how much I loved teaching and how happy I was at that school, with those kids, those teachers. I was twenty-six and finally knew who and what I was: a teacher.

But this time of the year *is* difficult. Kids come back from Spring Break all hopped up, no other breaks in sight as they look across the long desert of the months ahead and see only testing and projects, a regular obstacle course of challenges they must overcome in order to reach the cool water of summer. What is difficult for them is, however, rarely less difficult for us, as this letter I wrote to a colleague recently shows:

Hi Elaine,

I wish what was going on in class right now was as orderly and good as what has been going on in my own head as I read the books we are teaching (Conrad and Kafka). I've really found my reading satisfying lately but it hasn't carried over as neatly into the classroom. Am hoping we can get some sustainable traction for the rest of the week starting tomorrow!

Jim

Elaine, who is a master teacher and a real mentor of mine (in fact, she is the one who helped me get hired here years ago), wrote to me in much the same way I have written to you at times, which reminded me that we all need guides no matter how far along on this journey we are. You would like to imagine that you will get it right by the time you have taught as long as Elaine has (she will retire next year), but the truth is we don't, we just get better at embracing the complexities and enduring the challenges as we search for solutions to the latest problems. Here is what Elaine wrote in response to my letter:

Hi,

A long view from a veteran: The phenomena you are describing ought not to be viewed in the context of spring fatigue. This is the worst part of the year to be teaching seniors. The reasons? They are awaiting news from colleges; they are reading some very difficult, heavy literature; they want to be out of high school; they don't necessarily want to do the required work; they are looking tired (reasons I'm not sure of); they need a vacation; some of them are taking too many days away from school and are hence disconnected from the daily ebb and flow.

For years I took this all quite personally. The dialogue in my head: I'm not a good teacher; I can't engage them; while enthralled by the literature, I am often overwhelmed by its complexity; I haven't taught them how to write; they don't know how to read poetry and it's my fault, ad infinitum.

The transaction is feeling anything but neat. I'm right here with ya.

Elaine

I can't tell you how much I appreciated Elaine's words. She put in words some emotions and thoughts I didn't even realize I was experiencing until I read them!

It is the very mess of this process called education that nonetheless fascinates me, for even as I've been feeling all that Elaine captured, wonderful things have been unfolding in the beginning stages of the end. Remember the Monroe brothers I wrote to you about a while back? So many good things have grown out of that difficult but honest exchange. Some time after the field trip to Berkeley, I had the kids write about the experience. Since Tyler didn't go, I had him write me a letter about how I handled it and how he felt about it. He wrote:

Dear Mr. Burke,

I was not allowed to go on the field trip last Tuesday because I didn't pay enough attention in class and I wasn't very reliable. It taught me a valuable lesson. It really helped me realize that I have to work and earn something that I want, that it doesn't just come to me. I also realized that I can't just get away with not doing my homework.

Not being able to go taught me that I need to work harder and dedicate myself to things to help me get through struggles in my life. Everyone else was able to go besides me and that made me think a lot also. But I'm glad you didn't let me go. It helped me as a person.

Thank you,
Tyler Monroe

His twin brother, Tim, speaking at the end of our semesterlong Toastmasters International Youth Leadership Program (Toastmasters is a public-speaking organization), gave this short but generous speech as part of the final ceremony:

Hi my name is Tim Monroe, and today I am going to talk to you about Toastmasters, and how I think Toastmasters helped not just me but everybody else in this class. When Toastmasters first began, I did not have any confidence in myself to get up and give a speech. As the weeks went on, I looked and paid attention more. As time went on, I progressed to become a better speaker.

I would like to thank Mr. Burke for all that he has done for us. He comes every day with something new and exciting to teach us. He saw where all of us were at in the beginning and from then on he picked and poked at us to become the speakers we are today. Mr. Burke teaches us how to reach down further and go for the unthinkable. He shows us how to become someone we did not know we were.

This is what we look for as we reach for the end of the year: evidence of growth, change, improvement, not just as students but as people. In the days and weeks ahead, give them opportunities to prove themselves, create occasions that can inspire pride and the realization that they are more than they were when they walked into your class. Through the storm of demands and distractions to come, watch for (or create) some kind of intellectual rite of passage that will give them a sense of accomplishment in your class. Such challenges give them a chance to stand and deliver, to rise to the occasion, an experience that confirms what the Roman philosopher Seneca wrote two thousand years ago: "If a man is to know himself, he must be tested. No one finds out what he can do except by trying." A source closer to your own faith says this: "Suffering produces endurance, and endurance produces character, and character produces hope, and hope does not disappoint us" (Rom. 5:3–5).

So I will end with the ultimate good news, the greatest ending to one of the many stories of this year, and one which surely embodies all I was just saying about trials: Alyssa, the girl who was in that terrible accident, who by all the laws of physics and medicine should have died, is home, is walking (with great difficulty and much pain and the help of some kind of body brace, no doubt), and is feeling so well that she was able to call me last week to ask what she should be reading. I suggested she read Lance Armstrong's memoir, *It's Not About the Bike*.[2] Being a serious athlete (the college she accepted has promised to honor her scholarship even if she can't run next year), she needs to know that she can overcome this trauma and learn from it. She needs to know what Lance Armstrong learned from his experience with cancer, what everyone learns from facing and overcoming what they thought they could not:

> People ask me why I ride my bike for six hours a day; what is the pleasure? The answer is that I don't do it for the pleasure. I do it for the pain. In my most painful moments on the bike, I am at my most self-aware and self-defining. There is a point in every race when a rider encounters the real opponent and realizes that it's . . . himself. You might say pain is my chosen way of exploring the human heart.
>
> That pain is temporary. It may last a minute, or an hour, or a day, or a year, but eventually it subsides. And when it does, something else takes its place, and that thing might be called a greater space for happiness. We

have unrealized capacities that only emerge in crisis—capacities for enduring, for living, for hoping, for caring, for enjoying. Each time we overcome pain, I believe that we grow.

Cancer was the making of me: Through it I became a more compassionate, complete, and intelligent man, and therefore a more alive one. So that's why I ride, and why I ride hard. Because it makes me hurt, and so it makes me happy.[3]

So hold on, Joy, and work hard, teach well, and know that success is yours for this first year. I went out on a long bike ride Saturday. It was beautiful; the California coast receded into the distance as I turned the corner and headed toward the road that would bring me back to the Golden Gate Bridge and ultimately home. I had never taken this route before; it was all new to me, just as every day is still new to you. Turning that last corner, I found myself looking at one long steep hill ahead of me, but I rode it, pushed myself, allowing myself to look not at the top but only a few feet ahead of me, thus giving me a recurring sense of movement and achievement, which was rewarded by the breeze on the bridge as I eased my way home. You're just about up that hill and will soon be on the bridge that leads to the summer, when you can rest and look back and take the time you need to learn all that this year has to teach you when you have the time and patience to listen.

Your colleague,

Jim

☙

Dear Joy:

The only blessing of all this week's lost time was the time we found today to talk during lunch. Strange that we have had this conversation going on all year and yet never truly have had more than two minutes between the end of my period and the beginning of yours to talk (while you hastily erased my messy handwriting all over the whiteboard and I packed up to get out). While driving home, I thought about what you said, the question you asked, and it seemed like an "intended encounter" (a phrase I heard a man use last weekend while down in Alabama).

That you ask a question near the end of the year that troubled you in the beginning of the year shows you how enduring these challenges are and will remain, for each year presents new dilemmas, as will the seasons of your life to come.

Let me first tell you about the Well Words. In *The Teacher's Daybook*, a personal and professional planner I created (and use myself), I decided that everyone, no matter how busy they are, could find time to read and think about *one* word a week, especially a word that might help them find a bit of that missing balance in life.[1] The idea is rather simple: each week, take a Well Word (see Figure 22.1) and try to keep it in mind, follow its invitation, let it remind you what will help you find or keep the balance you need to teach well, enjoy your life outside of school, and sustain your commitment to being a teacher. There are even four blank boxes for you to fill in the words you need most, which I may have missed.

What follows is a rather detailed response to your question about how I "do it all." Don Graves, one of our profession's true masters, wrote a book a few years ago called *The Energy to Teach*, a book I discussed briefly, I believe in one of the first letters. The pages that follow refer to a teacher named Jack, but I am, in fact, that teacher; so the schedule you'll see outlines

Relax	Connect	Listen	Exercise	Celebrate	Challenge
Eat (well)	Join	Trust	Give	Learn	Wait
Love	Refuse	Accept	Try	Remember	Praise
Appreciate	Balance	Imagine	Contribute	Thank	Clarify
Grow	Respect	Risk	Practice	Honor	Eliminate
Confront	Change	Ask	Renew	Experience	Participate
Enjoy	Choose	Create	Forgive	Express	Notice
Laugh	Engage	Smile	Simplify	Entertain	
Delegate	Limit	Breathe	Toss	Reward	

FIGURE 22.1

the minutes of my days. What was especially important to me when I did the self-study Don mentions was the analysis of what takes energy and what gives it. Nothing that I can recall learning in recent years helps me more to keep and find my balance when I lose it (as I have lately at times). You ask why I write these letters? They give me tremendous energy, as all creative acts do. So read the following excerpt from Don's book, keeping in mind that "Jack" is me and "Sandy" is my wife, Susan. True, it was a few years ago, but I was by that time doing everything I do now—I had three kids, taught full-time, wrote books, and so on.

> INVITATION: Maintain a one-week record of events in your life both in school and at home. Rate these events or incidents for: energy giving, energy taking, and a waste of time.

> Invitations in this book allow you to carry out various assignments to give you more insight into the subject of human energy, yours and others. Most of the time, these exercises will apply directly to your life. I will do these assignments with you or show others who have tried them. It is important to maintain your journal or record keeping for at least a week. One or two days doesn't allow enough time to accommodate the ups and downs of a roller-coaster week. The relationship between home and school may require even more time. One week of recordings may not be enough to give you the perspectives you need. Still, just recording and analyzing for one week will give you a mental framework to continue to think about the energy issue.

I asked six of the teacher participants in my study of energy to keep a weeklong diary in response to my main research question, "What gives you energy, takes it away, and for you is a waste of time?" They kept a detailed record of everything they did at home and at school for one complete week, including Saturday and Sunday. Each rated their entries with their best estimates of what took or gave energy and was a waste of time. They often stopped and gave lengthy written analyses for making their decisions. All of the participants had responsibilities at home. I included the weekends because no one ever "just teaches" and no one lives at home without responsibilities or is "just a parent." The two worlds of home and school intersect and need to be considered together and apart.

A GLIMPSE INTO TEACHERS' LIVES
Each of the teachers used a slightly different approach to record and evaluate how he or she used time and interpreted the meaning of the evidence. I share these data now in preparation for your own examinations of your week. The first teacher, "Jack," a high-school English teacher, introduced a new category—neutral—in which he felt he could not get a reading on whether it took or gave energy. I share his record keeping, two days back-to-back: one for Sunday, and the other for Monday:

Code: AE: Add energy, TE: Take energy, N: neutral, WE: wastes energy.

Sunday: At Home
   9:00:   Awaken, plans for the day. N
   9:15:   Read paper and breakfast. N
   9:30:   Read essays. N
   9:45:   Further discussion about day. N
   9:50:   Grade papers. N
   10:20: Errand in neighborhood: bank, shopping for food. N
   10:50: Pack, etc. to get out the door for day's adventure, make sandwiches. TE
   11:10: Neighbors show up with presents for boys, interrupts prep for trip. TE
   11:30: Eddie has meltdown in van (last 30 min; entirely about having to sit in back seat). TE
   11:30: Drive to Eli's. TE
   11:50: Drive to Point (45 min. drive in which Eddie continues to be difficult). TE
   12:35: Picnic at Point—sunny, beautiful; had been gray and foggy. AE
   12:55: Watch three boys play @ park while Sandy (wife) stays at picnic site with baby. AE

1:20: Sat with Sandy and talked about parenting/Littleton/evil while kids played @ playground. AE

2:00: Walk along beach, through forest talking with Sandy with kids ahead of us looking for rocks and shells. AE
NOTE: This Point where we picnic is new to us and the new experience gives energy. AE

2:45: Stop at Point museum for snack after walk. N

2:55: Went through museum: interactive exhibits with kids. AE

3:55: Walk all the way back to retrieve van because kids too tired. AE

4:05: Wait outside museum with van while they finish museum. N

4:10: Drive home. N

4:30: Stop off in town where I teach for coffee and ice cream and I run into a student of mine. AE

4:45: Drive home while Sandy and I talk some more. AE

6:00: Check e-mail, unpack from the day. N

6:15: Shower. AE

6:25: Dinner during which Sandy and I talk about summer plans and finances. AE

7:00: To playground with Walter to watch/help him practice riding his bike. AE

7:30: On to computer network to read, edit, post out to group. N

8:00: Sidetracked into a few different projects—when I should be doing schoolwork. TE

9:00: Schoolwork with intermittent time on NET. TE

Midnight: Back up work and close day with a few poems. N

Monday: School Day

5:50: Wake up to alarm and son asking for breakfast. When I say I'll get it he won't let me because he "wants mommy to get it." TE

6:00: Check e-mail before leaving. N

6:05: Make lunch. N

6:10: Stop by donut shop for coffee and donut I eat as I drive to work. N

6:15–6:55: Drive to work during which time I listen to books on tape. N

6:55–8:00: School before anyone else so I can copy, set up, be available to students. About 15 students meet in my room every morning to talk, work, hang out. AE

7:45: Get mail, sample page layouts. AE

8:00: Period 1: Work well, all prep pays off—competence energizes. AE

8:20:   Assumption regarding work due is wrong. TE

10:05:   Former student comes by for advice. We talk for 15 min./ being valued and helpful. AE

10:20:   Prep period, work on papers. TE

10:35:   Work interrupted by student with questions about his project after which I return to work. TE

10:50:   Go to copy exemplars from assignment I've been grading. Can't find them. WE

11:15–12:10: Teaching fourth period. N

12:15–1:00:   Lunch alone reading *New Yorker.* N

1:05–2:05:   Junior class in library during which librarian drones on about how to use the library (TE) and my conferences with students. AE

2:05–3:00:   6th period. Jose (TE), conferences. AE

3:05:   Federico comes in for conference. TE

3:15:   Walk to office to check box before leaving. AE

3:20:   Humorous talk with colleague. AE

3:30:   Car won't start at first. TE

3:45:   Stop for snack for the drive. N

3:50–4:30:   Drive home. WE

4:30–4:45:   Check e-mail. N

4:45–6:30:   Nap, unusual to do this. AE

6:35:   Dinner with Sandy while we talk about $180 bill from plumber. TE

6:45:   Work with Sandy to help Eddie on homework assignment. N

7:00:   Go through mail, set up work for evening. N

7:30:   Take truck to mechanic for repair and walk eight blocks home. TE
          On way home see police officer and ask him to check on kid in neighborhood who may be dealing drugs or bringing trouble. AE

8:00:   Home to work on planning for tomorrow. TE

8:30:   Realize I left crucial papers at school (i.e., to help me with planning). TE

8:40–11:45:   Paperwork—student papers. TE/AE

11:45–12:00: Tried to watch a former student's multimedia project but couldn't get it to download. WE

12:05–12:45: Done with work, I read a few poems & Pinsky's *Sounds of Poetry* because I am challenging self, learning. AE

12:45:   To bed.

Jack then reviewed his recordings for the week then reflected on the meaning of what he had seen. Jack liked what he saw, though he was objective about the many mundane things that filled his life:

> I found myself thinking often about the story of Sysiphus from Camus, about how everyone has to push the rock up the mountain (thus taking energy) and it is only in the shadow of that pushing, in the hours it takes for him to walk down the mountain, in the lull of the work he must do, that he gets to think about what he wants to. So much of the week I charted my life seemed divided into those moments when I did what I *had* to do versus what I *wanted* or even *needed* to do. In short, I felt achievements—as a reader, husband, father, teacher, human—gave me energy; demands, especially from those whose tradition is to take, take energy.
>
> Certain people I find I associate with energy—i.e., I have come to expect they will fuel me, somehow feed me: Jerry, my colleague with whom I discuss poetry almost daily; we allow each other the power of an identity other than the teacher we both know we are: to each other we give permission to be the poets we both also call ourselves. My wife, sometimes from just being with her, other times from talking with her, still others from just thinking about her, she completes me, guides me, accompanies me, I have no equivalent friend nor any other who can fill me so full so fast. My editor, whose confidence in me, inspires in me a belief in myself that could power a car for the energy she summons. My students, past and present, the NET, my personal online community which exists through me, a responsibility and creation that prides me through my days despite its rather mundane demands.
>
> While I am trying to be precise in my notes there are certain habits and rituals I cannot capture in such minutiae:
>
> • Constantly punctuating most activities in any setting with notes on 3 × 5 cards for books and articles.
>
> • While waiting anywhere for more than a minute or two I might take out my Palm Pilot and sort through to-do's, make notes, read from the book or magazine I carry with me (usually poetry).
>
> • While working in office, take intermittent breaks from work to: cleanse palate with a poem; listen to music; jot ideas for chapters and projects on the whiteboards in the office; back away from work to just "think" for a few minutes; miscellaneous maintenance activities within the office; check e-mail on the NET; check my Web site to see if the student who manages it has incorporated the changes I suggested.

After surveying the minutiae of his recordings, Jack steps back to consider the nature of his life. He feels in control and is happy with the balance of his life. He knows there are some positive elements in his life that he wishes he could increase. I'm sure there are days when he wishes he could do nothing but read and write poetry. Nevertheless, as a father/husband/teacher/writer, he knows there are responsibilities he needs and wants to maintain. He is pleased that he has turned energy-taking events into energy-giving events. I refer to the squalling in the car en route to a family picnic that was turned into an energy giver on arrival at the park on Sunday.

He is also aware that he maintains a constant intellectual challenge through his 3 × 5 cards, the reading of poetry, writing notes on the dashboard of his car, or listening to books on tape while driving to work. Jack has high focus about the direction of his life and therefore knows better how he will maintain a constant high-energy climate as well as how to turn normally negative forces into positive ones. He has a strong relationship with Jerry, his teaching colleague and poet. I am reminded that if there is enough depth to a community of two, it supplies enough professional energy for both. Too many times people lament that their school or department gives them little professional energy. But, the data in this study show that one significant relationship is enough to sustain anyone professionally.

What gives me energy now, at this point in the year, is the promise of improvement next year. Designers often tell users of their products to create what they call bug lists (i.e., a list of what "bugs" them when they use a product). Thus this morning, while the kids took state tests and my AP kids took a practice AP test, I made a bug list for the classes I teach (and will teach again next year), for all our attention now begins to drift toward not the inevitable ending of this semester but the beginning of the fall, something you can't do because you don't know what you will teach, where you will be, and how to finish *this* year yet. . . . Within thirty minutes I had made a two-page list of all the things I want to "fix," improve, or otherwise do better next year. In short, I have run the experiment of this year, told the story, run the program—and it has ended where it has, an ending made of mixed results sprung from best intentions and well-made plans that make this year little more than the next draft in the story of my work. So the bug list reads a bit like a list of what to prune; as the Benedictines say (or so I read in yesterday's *Wall Street Journal*, that great chronicle of our country's spiritual health) "pruned: it grows again." I like that; I feel, especially in my

AP class, that I *have* been pruned this year as never before, and pruned the way *I* prune a tree: leaving me to wonder how it will ever grow back and find the strength it needs to blossom again. Yet I know I will grow back, for already my bug list reminds me of all I can do, what I can learn so that I might return in the fall and revise not only my curriculum but myself.

I end with one last comment about the energy to do it all. First, no one does it all; they learn to do what matters most, to do what comes next, to avoid what doesn't matter or to do it in the most efficient way without losing much will in the completion of the task. If you work in isolation, as we too often do, you can get lost within the work, inside yourself, and not find your way out. This is why you must do things that take you out of the cycle of work and make room for rest and rejuvenation. For example, I can tell you that the first Monday night of every month next school year, I will be having a nice dinner with my wife and going to hear a great talk by such people as Bill Moyers and Colin Powell because we just bought tickets to a speaker series. We make time for what matters. This will ensure that I have a good conversation with my wife, some adult time away from our wonderful children, an evening of stimulating ideas for dessert, and a night off from doing teacher work, all of which will restore me and send me back to school the next morning with ideas to share that will make me a more interesting teacher because I will be a healthier and more interesting person.

We must also, however, get out of our own experience and classroom by joining the larger conversation that goes on within the profession. For me, this has meant going to conventions, reading professional journals, and maintaining online professional discussions with colleagues I have met at these conventions. For you have not taken a job, but rather joined a profession, entered a community, a tradition that has been going on for several millennia at this point. I'm *sure* when Socrates held his first class under an acacia tree, he asked the class a question and no one responded; I'm sure they just looked at their sandals or picked lint out of their belly buttons the way my kids did when I began teaching. You have, without entirely knowing it, joined that conversation through these letters, asking me to think about things just as I, through my books and articles, ask other teachers to think about their work and join in the conversation about that work with me. I received an extra copy of a journal I write for (*Voices from the Middle*) and wanted to pass it along to you as an invitation to that larger conversation. My column in this particular issue draws on my experiences as a student teacher but is inspired by the occasion of Louise Rosenblatt's death last month at one hundred. Imagine this: seventy-nine years older than you, this woman stood at NCTE last November to address a room filled with teachers she had guided through her books, her teaching, her *life*, coming out with her last book at *one hundred!* Here, then, is my column from the issue, which you might find helpful in light of what I have discussed in this letter.

VOICES

During the year I spent getting my teaching credential at San Francisco State University, two encounters marked that year as something special, though I only know this in hindsight. One of the people came to the campus to give a talk: Robert Scholes. He was just then beginning the work about textuality that would evolve into some of the most compelling thinking about our discipline. The other person I met not in person but through her book *The Reader, the Text, the Poem.* This second person, Louise Rosenblatt, came with something that not even Robert Scholes had: the passionate blessing of my mentor, Dorothy Petit. Dorothy Petit spoke of Louise Rosenblatt with a mix of passion and awe, respect and humility that was unusual for Dr. Petit.

It was not my good fortune to attend a school of education that was in any way accomplished, that did research or even had about it an air of urgency or importance. Indeed, when I asked when the commencement ceremony would be held, they simply said there was none. When I graduated, I left not with a diploma but something that would prove much more valuable over the years: the voices of a few people, Louise Rosenblatt's foremost among them, to provide the light and leadership as I fumbled my way into the profession.

In *Literature as Exploration*, Louise wrote: "A novel or poem or play remains merely ink spots on paper until a reader transforms them into a set of meaningful symbols." This captures the effect on me of her work and, more importantly, her example as not just a scholar and writer, but a leader and a voice insisting on the importance of literature, our work, and thus teachers. Her example *transformed* me and my understanding of my work, making me see that it involved so much more than merely teaching grammar or "literature."

Seeing her in person for the first time this past November at NCTE, I was amazed that such power, even at 100, could come from this small woman looking out over the hundreds of teachers at the Middle School Mosaic who stood to applaud their gratitude. I felt as though she were there to pass on to us the obligation she herself lived through her work. This is what I was thinking about—her example to us all—as I sat in my office this last week looking at her latest book, which arrived that afternoon, when an email chimed. Looking up, I saw only "Louise Rosenblatt" in the subject line. It was Kylene Beers announcing that Louise Rosenblatt had just died. Yet she will live on through her voice, her words, her example, her challenge to us all that, in an era guided by numbers, we should commit ourselves anew to the importance of creating thoughtful classrooms where students gather to transform "ink spots on paper . . . into meaningful symbols" so that those ink spots might, in turn, transform our students into the thoughtful citizens we dream they will become and which Louise Rosenblatt was for one hundred years.[3]

See you next week,

Jim

Dear Joy:
A Final Letter

⋋

Dear Joy:

I knew you had arrived as a teacher when I watched you handle Kaitlyn and her rat in your classroom the other day. It wasn't the way you responded to the rat but rather the way you handled the classroom as the girls freaked and the boys flocked in fascination. What struck me was the tone and confidence of your voice as you called out over the commotion: "All right, let's all find out why Kaitlyn has her rat with her today so we can ignore it and get down to work!" And when Jessica seemed closer to passing out than ignoring the rat, you just assured her that it was only a pet and wouldn't harm her. Then you went on to do exactly what you said: addressed the issue and got going with the class.

Even as I watched, I couldn't help thinking about Kaitlyn, who began high school last year (in my Academic Success class) in a puddle of tears, telling me about how her father had left her and her mother but was holding all her pets hostage in their house. She was desperate with worry about what would happen to her pets, no doubt a refuge from the troubles in her human habitat. Those were difficult days, culminating in her worries about how she and her mother would get by; I remember her telling me and her counselor through her choking sobs that she had given her mother the money she had saved up to buy a horse so they could buy groceries. And yet life endures, and we find ourselves on the other side of troubles we thought for sure would kill us. And so has she. As the poet Milosz wrote, "the heart does not die when one thinks it should, we smile, there is tea and bread on the table."

On most Sundays, I get up early and ride my bike south along the coast to Funston Point. Only the surfers and fishermen are out; the waves unfold in the fog along the beach. It is about a ten-mile ride that culminates in one final hill before I reach Funston Point. This is, for me, a somewhat sacred ride, and usually my favorite of the week. If it is windy, as it usually is, there are hangliders soaring through the skies at Funston. They launch themselves from a field nearby, the wind taking their bright wings aloft and sending them down the coast, out over the waters of the Pacific. When I see them in the months to come, I will think of you and how you have begun to soar, to carry yourself out over the waters that would take us all if we let them. And when I am there, at Funston, watching the ocean, the sky, the world awaken, I try always to offer my gratitude for all I have learned that week, all I have had the chance to do, for all the blessings of my family. I will add to those blessings this year I have shared with you; I'm grateful for all you gave me the chance to learn from and share with you. Thinking of such mornings, of the trials and triumphs of this year we have shared together, I say farewell for now with this poem from my most cherished poet of all, Czeslaw Milosz, who died after ninety years of bearing witness to the wonders this world:

GIFT

A day so happy.
Fog lifted early, I worked in the garden.
Hummingbirds were stopping over honeysuckle flowers
There was no thing on earth I wanted to possess.
I knew no one worth my envying him.
Whatever evil I had suffered, I forgot.
To think that once I was the same man did not embarrass me.
In my body I felt no pain.
When straightening up, I saw the blue sea and sails.[1]

Jim

Dear Jim:
A Final Letter

Dear Jim:

We survived! The school year at Burlingame High and Mills High is over. My thirty-minute commute to and from work is no more, my traveling between two high schools is finished, and feeling distant from both school communities is now over. Hurray! I am happy these aspects of my year ended, but I can't look back on last year without an overwhelming appreciation for all you did to support me as a new teacher. I am especially thankful because the new school year is about to begin and I am in need of all the advice you gave me.

I must admit I am sad that you will not be by my side when I need assistance this year. My dad was just watching the old Star Wars movies and I can't help but think of you as my Yoda. I am now on my own and I must "use the force" within me to survive and thrive at my new high school. Although I am not a "Jedi" teacher yet, I know, even amidst the sadness, there is a new confidence in my ability to teach. This confidence developed under your guidance and direction. Thank you for the books, the letters, and the life lessons you taught me this past year. It is exciting to think that by sharing your wisdom with me you are investing in hundreds of my future students! What an impact you've made this year and will continue to make in the years to come!

I am not sure if I mentioned this to you earlier, but your impact on me even filtered down to a particular student at Mills. I wrote a letter to you concerning the problems I was having with her in October. After writing her a letter and encouraging her, she improved some, but still struggled in all her classes. Ultimately she switched to the alternative school in the district. During the last month of school she came back to visit. She intentionally came to my class to thank me for my commitment to her and to express her gratitude for my assistance in school. She informed me that she was doing very well and enjoying the new environment at the alternative school. After *her visit I was walking on air and couldn't believe how my actions had influenced her so much. I find it amazing how much power I have over my students. Funny enough, my students have so much power over me, too. When they are discouraged, I feel it, and when they succeed, I feel it. Oh, the relationship we have with our students. Thank you for contributing to this success story.*

I must get back to preparing lessons, but I am struck by how much the last year prepared me for my beginnings at a new school. This new school year brings many changes—even adjustments in my schedule (I am teaching a few classes I didn't expect to teach!). And who knew I would work at the school I wrote to you about earlier in the year? My teacher muscles were exercised last year and are building resistance to the challenges that teachers face. I can do what I didn't think I could do. I understand my strength and ability because my mentor at Santa Cruz High started me off with fabulous guidance and you've carried on what she began. You both were willing to take a young teacher under your wing. From this nurturing I now have a knowledge bank within me that I can tap into when I need help. My questions will never end. Yet they can be answered in part by what I carry within me. Other answers will come from new mentors at my new school and from you!

I look forward to sharing what you've taught me with my students and other teachers who need the encouragement in their first years of teaching. Let the cycle of guidance and wisdom continue!

Your old roommate,

Joy

Notes

～

QUESTION 1

1. Covey, Stephen R. 2004. *The Seven Habits of Highly Effective People: Powerful Lessons of Personal Change.* New York: Free.

QUESTION 2

1. Atwell, Nancie. 1998. *In the Middle: New Understandings About Writing, Reading, and Learning.* Portsmouth, NH: Heinemann, p. 3.
2. Applebee, Arthur. 1996. *Curriculum as Conversation: Transforming Traditions of Teaching and Learning.* Chicago: University of Chicago Press.
3. Judith Langer has two books on this subject: *Effective Literacy Instruction: Building Successful Reading and Writing Programs* (Urbana, IL: National Council of Teachers of English, 2002) and *Getting to Excellent: How to Create Better Schools* (New York: Teachers College Press, 2004). You can also access Langer's research and various related reports online at the Center for English Learning and Achievement (CELA) website, http://cela.albany.edu.
4. Three books stand out: Parker Palmer's *Courage to Teach* (San Francisco: Jossey Bass, 1997), Don Graves' *Energy to Teach* (Portsmouth, NH: Heinemann, 2001), and my own *Teacher's Daybook* (Portsmouth, NH: Heinemann, 2005).

QUESTION 3

1. This quotation from the Roman philosopher Seneca appears in Tom Morris' wonderful book *True Success: A New Philosophy of Excellence* (New York: Berkeley, 1994), in which he studied why the Notre Dame football players were failing his philosophy class and what the great philosophers had to say about success. His result was the Seven Cs of Success, which he outlines in detail in this book.
2. Many have begun to examine the struggles of people engaged in demanding but creative work and the effects of those struggles that might undermine their performance. My favorite books on this subject are *The Energy to Teach*, by Don Graves (Portsmouth, NH: Heinemann, 2001); *The Power of Full Engagement*, by Jim Loehr and Tony Schwartz (New York: Free, 2003); and *The Seven Habits of Highly Effective People*, by Stephen Covey (New York: Free, 1989). Covey recently came out with a new book, *The Eighth Habit* (New York: Free, 2004), which adds important perspective to his other ideas, particularly his idea that we should "use our voice to help others find theirs."

3. Stafford, William. 1998. "Vocation." *The Way It Is: New and Selected Poems.* St. Paul, MN: Graywolf.

4. Steinbeck, John. 1955. "Like Captured Fireflies." *California Teachers' Association Journal* 51 (November): 6–9.

QUESTION 4

1. Jago, Carol. 2001. *Beyond Standards: Excellence in the High School English Classroom.* Portsmouth, NH: Heinemann.

2. Bransford, John D., Ann L. Brown, and Rodney R. Cocking. 2000. *How People Learn: Brain, Mind, Experience, and School.* Washington, DC: National Academy Press.

3. Heaney, Seamus. 1991. *The Cure at Troy: A Version of Sophocles' Philoctetes.* New York: Farrar, Straus and Giroux.

4. Tzu, Lao. 1992. *Tao Te Ching.* Trans. Stephen Mitchell. San Francisco: Perennial.

QUESTION 5

1. Piercy, Marge. 2003. "Seven of Pentacles." *Teaching with Fire: Poetry That Sustains the Courage to Teach.* San Francisco: Jossey-Bass.

2. Stafford, William. 1999. "Ask Me." *The Way It Is: New and Selected Poems.* St. Paul, MN: Graywolf.

3. The book that helped me understand this best was Sheridan Blau's *Literature Workshop: Teaching Texts and Their Readers* (Portsmouth, NH: Heinemann, 2003).

4. Burke, Jim. 2004. *School Smarts: The Four Cs of Academic Success.* Portsmouth, NH: Heinemann.

QUESTION 6

1. Burke, Jim. 2003. *The English Teacher's Companion: A Complete Guide to Classroom, Curriculum, and the Profession.* 2d ed. Portsmouth, NH: Heinemann.

2. Schmoker, Mike. 1999. *Results: The Key to Continuous School Improvement.* Alexandria, VA: Association of Supervision and Curriculum Development.

3. CATENet is an online forum (run by mailing listserver) I created years ago for language arts teachers. It is a community of about ten thousand teachers and leaders who share information about policy and practice. You can learn more about it by going to www.englishcompanion.com/catenet/catenet.html.

4. Personal correspondence from Leif Fearn, October 2, 2004. Leif Fearn and Nancy Farnan wrote an excellent book called *Interactions: Teaching Writing and the Language Arts* (Boston: Houghton Mifflin, 2001). While their book is about all aspects of writing, some have written specifically about handling the paper load. Two books in particular stand out: *Handling the Paperload*, edited by Jeff Golub (Urbana, IL: National Council of Teachers of English, 2005) and *Papers, Papers, Papers: An English Teacher's Survival Guide*, by Carol Jago (Portsmouth, NH: Heinemann, 2005).

5. Personal correspondence from Carol Jago, October 2, 2004.

6. Kids have a vested interest in their teachers being successful and effective. They know what they need and, if given the opportunity, will tell you in terms that can help. They

are especially helpful if they see, from previous experiences in your class, that you listen to, learn from, and put to use suggestions of theirs that make a difference.

7. For more information about the Weekly Paper, including the *Weekly Reader* digital textbook, assignment, and student samples, go to www.englishcompanion.com /room82/weeklyreader.html.

INTERLUDE 2

1. Zander, Rozamund Stone, and Benjamin Zander. 2000. *The Art of Possibility: Transforming Professional and Personal Life.* Boston: Harvard Business School Press.

QUESTION 7

1. Suzuki, Shunryu. 1970. *Zen Mind, Beginner's Mind.* New York: Walker/Weatherhill. The poet Rainer Marie Rilke also wrote with great appreciation for the importance of always approaching each task, or in his case each poem, as if you were a beginner. He discusses this idea and many others you might find interesting in his book *Letters to a Young Poet* (San Rafael, CA: New World Library, 1992).

2. *The Teacher's Daybook* (Portsmouth, NH: Heinemann, 2005) is a planner I created specifically for teachers. My goal was to produce something that would help us achieve better personal and professional balance amidst the swarm of demands we face throughout the school year. This need for balance becomes all the more important as you grow into the profession and take on new roles, develop important relationships outside of school, have children, or face added responsibilities for aging parents—all of which happens despite the incessant demands of teaching.

3. Gilbert, Jack. 1984. "The Abnormal Is Not Courage." *Monolithos.* St. Paul, MN: Graywolf.

4. The Continuum of Performance was discussed on pages 37–38.

5. Chase, Dawn. 2001. "The Basics of Classroom Management." *California English* (April): 2.

QUESTION 8

1. *Tuned in and Fired Up* (New Haven, CT: Yale University Press, 2003) is actually based on a yearlong study of my classroom by the author Sam Intrator.

2. Nye, Naomi Shihab. 2001. *What Have You Lost?* New York: HarperTempest.

3. Komunyakaa, Yusef. 2001. "The Deck." *Pleasure Dome: New and Collected Poems.* Middletown, CT: Wesleyan University Press, p. 404. Komunyakaa's poetry is remarkable in its diversity of subject. His poems also manage to be both accessible and challenging.

4. Stafford, William. 1999. "The Way It Is." *The Way It Is: New and Selected Poems.* St. Paul, MN: Graywolf.

5. In addition to *Teaching with Fire: Poetry That Sustains the Courage to Teach* (San Francisco: Jossey-Bass, 2003), Sam Intrator published a wonderful collection of personal narratives called *Stories of the Courage to Teach: Honoring the Teacher's Heart* (San Francisco: Jossey-Bass, 2002).

6. For more information about the National Endowment for the Humanities summer institutes, visit http://neh.gov/.

QUESTION 10

1. Phillips, Donald. 1993. *Lincoln on Leadership: Executive Strategies for Tough Times.* New York: Warner.
2. Triana, Richard. "What Makes a Good Teacher?" *Education Week* 18 (19): 34.
3. Osborn, Michael, and Suzanne Osborn. 1997. *Public Speaking.* 3d ed. Boston: Houghton Mifflin.

QUESTION 11

1. Burke, Jim. "At the Coliseum." Originally appeared in *Teacher Magazine* (March).

QUESTION 13

1. "Ten Secrets to Success." *Investor's Business Daily.* This feature appears daily in the paper and can be accessed online at www.hoffman.com/inthenews/articles/ibd_feb2069.htm
2. "Tame Your Inner Critic." *Investor's Business Daily.*

QUESTION 14

1. Burke, Jim. 2005. *ACCESSing School: Teaching Struggling Readers to Achieve Academic and Personal Success.* Portsmouth, NH: Heinemann.
2. Norman, Donald. 1993. *Things That Make Us Smart: Defending Human Attributes in the Age of the Machine.* Reading, MA: Addison-Wesley, p. 2251.
3. Snyder, Gary. 2005. "Axe Handles." *Axe Handles.* Emeryville, CA: Shoemaker & Hoard.

QUESTION 15

1. Rosenblatt, Louise. 1996. *Literature as Exploration.* New York: Modern Language Association, p. 17.

QUESTION 16

1. Fox, Matthew. 1995. *The Reinvention of Work: A New Vision of Livelihood for Our Time.* San Francisco: HarperSanFrancisco.
2. Gayles, Gloria Wade, ed. 2002. *In Praise of Our Teachers: A Multicultural Tribute to Those Who Inspired Us.* Boston: Beacon.
3. Ayers, William. 2001. *To Teach: The Journey of a Teacher.* 2d ed. New York: Teachers College Press.
4. Early on in my career I began calling students "Miss" and "Mr." on occasion. I don't do it all the time but do it regularly. Kids respond well to it; I suspect it makes them feel simultaneously respected and older, more mature. I don't make a big deal of it, but do use it, for example, in class discussions or on notes I write the kids. In some instances, it also helps to create a bit of distance, a more formal tone even as it simultaneously maintains an air of familiarity.

QUESTION 18

1. This poem has circulated for some time and is, so far as I can determine, without a known source to cite. I first encountered it through a friend who, upon entering his teaching credential program, was given it by his professor.

QUESTION 19

1. Gibbs, Nancy. 2005. "Parents Behaving Badly." *Time* 3.
2. Curwin, Richard, and Allen Mendler. 2000. *Discipline with Dignity.* Upper Saddle River, NJ: Prentice Hall.
3. While I advocate communicating honestly and openly with parents and kids, I am not reckless nor naïve: anything you write is a public record and can be used in a legal action. It is often best to sleep on it a night before sending any letters, especially those written in the heat of the moment.
4. Drucker, Peter. 2005. "Managing Oneself." *Harvard Business Review* (January).
5. Light, Richard. 2004. *Making the Most of College: Students Speak Their Minds.* Cambridge: Harvard University Press.

INTERLUDE 8

1. Kipling, Rudyard. 1999. "If." *The Collected Poems of Rudyard Kipling.* Lincolnwood, IL: NTC/Contemporary Publishing Company.

QUESTION 21

1. Eliot, T. S. 1953. "Little Giddings." *The Collected Poems of T. S. Eliot.* New York: Harcourt.
2. Armstrong, Lance. 2001. *It's Not About the Bike: My Journey Back to Life.* New York: Berkley Trade.
3. Armstrong, Lance. 2001. "Back in the Saddle." *Forbes ASAP* (December 3).

QUESTION 22

1. Burke, Jim. 2005. *The Teacher's Daybook.* Portsmouth, NH: Heinemann.
2. Graves, Don. 2001. *The Energy to Teach.* Portsmouth, NH: Heinemann.
3. Burke, Jim. 2005. "Voices." *Voices from the Middle.* National Council of Teachers of English (March).

DEAR JOY: A FINAL LETTER

1. Milosz, Czeslaw. 2003. "The Gift," *New and Collected Poems: 1931–2001.* New York: Ecco.

Preventing/Minimizing/Handling Disruptions: The Basics of Classroom Management

BY DAWN CHASE

~

Since 1997, I have supervised student teachers and interns in English, first for San Jose State, currently for Stanford. Most of the beginning teachers I've worked with have at least an adequate command of their subject; many have been outstanding in their academic preparation. Where they are likely to need help is in establishing and maintaining a classroom environment conducive to learning. Some are interns or teaching under contract on emergency credentials, responsible for two, three, even five classes a day, with little preparation beyond their undergraduate course work. Often they've been hired after school has started and so have missed whatever orientation the school has provided. On-site support varies widely, from informal help offered by sympathetic colleagues to more systematic mentoring under programs such as BTSA. Accustomed to university classes, they often make assumptions that are inappropriate when trying to teach 30 to 150 or more adolescents.

What follows is a sort of primer based on exemplary practices as well as on mistakes I've made and observed during 35 years in middle and high school English classrooms. While much of this will seem obvious to experienced teachers, many of these suggestions are not so obvious to beginners. Here is what I tell beginning teachers to help their development as classroom managers:

Rules matter. They say that what we are doing in this classroom is serious and important. Effective teachers are clear about academic and behavioral expectations. Their students understand those expectations and know that there will be fair and reasonable consequences for not meeting them, but also that the teacher will listen to their views and be open to their suggestions.

I. Steps to take before asking for help:

A. At the beginning of the year, involve the class in agreeing on rules you and they can live with. Keep these simple and enforceable.

B. Learn students' names and establish routines early. Plan a quiet activity—journals, a quiz, daily oral language drill—for the beginning of class. This frees you to take attendance and deal with other routine chores.

C. Be prepared. Know what you will do, why you are doing it, what students will do, how long each activity should take. Plan more than you think you'll be able to accomplish. Allow less time than you think students will need. Write all this, including times, into your lesson plan. Then, be flexible about what actually goes on during class. You might use all of it, some of it, or very little, but it will increase your confidence to know where you intend to go next.

D. Now that you know where you're going, be sure that students know it too. Be clear and concise in giving directions, and check students' understanding frequently, perhaps by asking them to repeat what you've just said. Have daily and weekly agendas on the board or in another accessible location.

E. When possible, give kids choices—projects, due dates, books the class will read can be subject to negotiation. Number of tardies, passes out of class, late homework can also be discussed, agreed upon, and posted or distributed as a handout. Know your school's policies on such issues and be sure yours are in line with these.

F. At least at first, assign seats. This helps you learn names more quickly. Alphabetically is easiest, but do it backwards so the Z-names are in the front. (Often these kids have been in the back row all their lives!) Changes the seating chart when you need to, and adjust the seating arrangements to the activity; e.g., in a circle for whole-class discussions or Socratic seminars, in rows for tests and quizzes, in small circles for cooperative learning.

G. Assign students to groups, using criteria appropriate to the task. In a graduate seminar, the professor can tell the class to turn to the next person and talk about the point just covered. Middle and high school students need far more structure and direction; assign roles, limit time, require a product to be handed in.

H. Move around the room. A seated teacher is an invitation to misbehavior. Be aware of students' body language. Stand close to any student who appears inattentive. Insist on attention when you or others are speaking.

I. Write key words of student questions/comments on the board or overhead. This validates their contributions in a very powerful way.

J. Deal firmly but unobtrusively with individual problems. Never argue with a kid about his/her behavior. Instead:

1. Give a brief, quiet reminder at the student's desk.
2. Change his/her seat.
3. Send student outside with directions to stay where you can see him/her. When the rest of the class is working, speak to the student in the hall.
4. Detain the student after school or during lunch, unless this is worse punishment for you than it is for the kid. Assign some useful chore or require reading or study during detention.
5. Call home, but be prepared for problems. Language difficulties, parental helplessness, overly punitive responses are all possibilities, but they can also provide useful information.
6. Keep a record of steps taken and when. This adds credibility to a referral if you need to write one. The record can be as simple as post-it notes in the grade book.

K. To deal with situations involving the whole class:

1. Plan a reward for the class if everyone behaves well. Perhaps provide, or have the kids provide, refreshments occasionally. Otherwise, no food or drink in class; it should be a special treat.
2. If you're really angry, let them know it, but do so in an adult way. Don't let it become a confrontation on their level, and reserve expressions of anger for really serious situations.

3. If an entire class continues to misbehave, try silent seat work. Grammar exercises and worksheets won't hurt them and can give them time to reflect on why you're assigning these. When they're ready to cooperate, discuss possible solutions with them. Ask them to offer suggestions for how to improve the learning environment.

L. To minimize cheating:

   1. Let students know that you are familiar with Internet sites on topics they are studying.
   2. Require them to write first drafts in class. Collect these at the end of the hour.
   3. Be sure that kids know what plagiarism is and why it is wrong.
   4. If you suspect plagiarism, meet to discuss the paper. Ask the student to explain difficult words and ideas.
   5. During tests, separate students from each other and require them to clear their desks. Move around or stay at the back of the room while they work.
   6. Prepare different forms of the same test, keeping the same questions but scrambling their order. Make at least part of the test essay; this is good practice, and it makes cheating less likely.
   7. Occasionally make tests a collaborative effort, especially when kids are working well in groups. Be sensitive to fairness issues, with this as well with all group work. Don't let the same kids do all the work, all the time.

II. Try to handle most problems yourself, but realize that sometimes kids will not cooperate despite your best efforts.

ASK FOR HELP WHEN YOU NEED IT.

In the event of a major problem—serious defiance or threats, fighting, suspected drug or weapons possession—call or send for help immediately.

A. Talk to other teachers and coaches. Find a mentor/friend, not necessarily the official or assigned mentor.
B. Learn the policies at your school on such issues as tardiness, unacceptable language, disrupting class, etc. Get to know the person in charge of discipline before problems arise.

C. If you have to send a student to the office, document what the kid has done and what steps you've taken to correct the problem.

D. If an entire class consistently misbehaves, ask the administrator in charge of discipline to speak to the class. With him or her, work out a plan for improving the class environment. Remember, you've been keeping a record of problems. With this in hand, you won't as readily be suspected of crying wolf.

E. Realize that some problems are beyond our control. We are not parole officers or psychotherapists. If you've done everything a responsible adult can do and nothing seems to be working, don't blame yourself. Get help from appropriate sources, starting with the local administration.

From *California ENGLISH*, April 2001. Reprinted with permission.

Action Planner

	Description of Steps	Your Notes
1.	**Define the problem.** Write the problem in language that is clear, specific, and concise. Focus on what a student or class does not do or understand, something that prevents their success.	
2.	**Generate possible causes.** List all the possible causes or sources of this problem; include even those that seem not to apply but with other students might.	
3.	**Describe desired behavior or outcome.** Provide a precise description of the behavior or action the student must show or do to succeed in the situation (e.g., your class, this assignment).	
4.	**Identify possible obstacles to success.** Choose from the following: commitment; knowledge; skills; stamina; adaptability; elasticity. If these don't help, generate your own.	
5.	**Determine necessary resources.** List resources—people, materials, facilities—you need to effectively help the student make the necessary changes. "Resources" do *not* include info, lessons, or skills they must learn.	
6.	**Identify the necessary knowledge.** What do *you* need to know and believe to help this student succeed? What does the student need to know and believe to be able to succeed? What's the best way to learn this?	

The Four Cs of Academic Success

Commitment	Content
Commitment describes the extent to which students care about the work and maintain consistency in their attempt to succeed.	*Content* refers to information or processes students must know to complete a task or succeed on an assignment in class.

Key aspects of **commitment** are:
• *Emotional investment:* Refers to how much students care about their success and the quality of their work on this assignment or performance
• *Effort:* Some students resist making a serious effort when they do not believe they can succeed. Without such effort, neither success nor improvement is possible
• *Consistency:* Everyone can be great or make heroic efforts for a day or even a week; real, sustainable success in a class or on large assignments requires consistent hard work and "quality conscience"
• *Faith:* Students must believe that the effort they make will eventually lead to the result or success they seek. Faith applies to a method or means by which they hope to achieve success
• *Permission:* Students must give themselves permission to learn and work hard and others permission to teach and support them if they are to improve and succeed.
	Content knowledge includes:
	• *Discipline- or subject-specific matter* such as names, concepts, and terms
	• *Cultural reference points* not specifically related to the subject but necessary to understand the material, such as:
	  • People
	  • Events
	  • Trends
	  • Ideas
	  • Dates
	• *Conventions* related to documents, procedures, genres, or experiences
	• *Features, cues, or other signals* that convey meaning during a process or within a text.
	• *Language* needed to complete or understand the task
	• *Procedures* used during the course of the task or assignment.

Competencies	Capacities
Competencies are those skills students need to be able to complete the assignment or succeed at some task.	*Capacities* account for the quantifiable aspects of performance; students can have great skills but lack the capacity to fully employ those skills.
Representative, general **competencies** include the ability to: • *Generate* ideas, solutions, and interpretations that will lead to the successful completion of the task • *Manage* resources (time, people, and materials) needed to complete the task; refers also to the ability to govern oneself • *Communicate* ideas and information to complete and convey results of the work • *Evaluate* and *make decisions* based on information needed to complete the assignment or succeed at the task • *Learn* while completing the assignment so students can improve their performance on similar assignments in the future • *Use* a range of tools and strategies to solve the problems they encounter.	Primary **capacities** related to academic performance include: • *Speed* with which students can perform one or more tasks needed to complete the assignment or performance • *Stamina* required to maintain the requisite level of performance; includes physical and mental stamina • *Fluency* needed to handle problems or interpret ideas that vary from students' past experience or learning • *Dexterity*, which allows students, when needed, to do more than one task at the same time (aka multitasking) • *Memory*, so students can draw on useful background information or store information needed for subsequent tasks included in the assignment • *Resiliency* needed to persevere despite initial or periodic obstacles to success on the assignment or performance • Confidence in their ideas, methods, skills, and overall abilities related to this task.

From *School Smarts: The Four Cs of Academic Success*, by Jim Burke, © 2004 (Heinemann: Portsmouth, NH).